plant to plate

GAZ OAKLEY

Delicious and Versatile
Plant-Forward Recipes

Photography by Tom Kong
with Gaz Oakley, Oliver Biggs
& Matthew Williams

Quadrille

Growth

My journey into the world of cooking started at a very young age. It began by watching my dad cook our dinners, seeing him sharpen knives, perfect his knife skills and tossing ingredients into hot pans. To me, the creativity, knives and flames seemed fun. There was always a cooking show of some sort on the TV too, with chefs like Rick Stein, Keith Floyd or Gordon Ramsey. My world revolved around food, it seemed. We would go to France a lot in the summer holidays and, although they weren't foodie trips (more like caravan-camping holidays), we would take road trips through French towns, stopping off at boulangeries for fresh bread and produce at the Sunday markets. The romanticism the French had for food captivated me.

After a few years of learning the kitchen basics at home with my dad, I was hooked. I knew all I wanted to be was a chef, so that's what I did. Aged fifteen, I got a part-time job at a beautiful hotel restaurant and had dreams of becoming the youngest ever chef to obtain three Michelin stars, hopefully taking the crown from my hero Marco Pierre White... At sixteen I left school and went full time in the kitchen. I soaked up as much knowledge as possible from the chefs around me and spent all my waking hours working. It was tough, but the thrill, creativity and skills I was quickly gaining was all worth it.

I loved being adventurous with food from a very young age, but I always cared most about what the diners thought. I'd pester waiters for feedback from the guests and often poke my head out of the

kitchen, hoping to see satisfaction on faces. I'd spend far too much time looking through online reviews of the restaurants I worked at to see if anyone had mentioned any of the dishes I'd made.

I look back on these years with admiration for my young self. It took a lot of dedication and drive to sacrifice my late teens and early twenties to the kitchen. While all my friends were out partying, meeting girls and seeing the world, I was burning out after 80+ hour weeks from the age of sixteen.

But this was my training, and although I didn't end up going after those Michelin stars (not yet anyway), I did gain a wealth of experience in cooking, running a restaurant, efficiency, work ethic and team work. I also made lifelong friends because, when you spend so much time together in kitchens, the brigade becomes almost like family.

During these years I don't think I deeply appreciated produce, certainly not how I do now. I remember deliveries would turn up with beautiful, seasonal produce and to me it just looked like, well, veg! At the time, it didn't excite me as much as the fresh pigeons or venison that arrived at the restaurant. But that all changed a few years ago.

After taking some time out of the kitchen, I changed my whole lifestyle and career. I pivoted my cooking skills to the social media world and I began making my own cooking show for YouTube. Somehow, it became a hit and, as of 2025, there are nearly 3 million people from all around the world watching me talk about food on some sort of social media platform. This career has taken me across the globe, allowed me to meet incredible people and learn so much about the food culture of others. I've even featured on the legendary Rick Stein's *Food Stories* show, which was an unbelievable moment for me and my dad after so many years watching him on TV.

I believe one of the reasons I was invited to be on Rick's show was because of a big transition I decided to make a few years ago. I'd been living in London for a few years, making my cooking show from my apartment, when the Covid lockdown hit. After months and months of feeling isolated, helpless and totally dependent on 'the system', I knew I had to make a change. I needed a sense of nature, and I needed to reconnect the relationship between myself and food. I started watching videos online about how to grow my own food and began searching for places to live back in my homeland of Wales. After a few months, I found a place around an hour away from the city I grew up in. I decided to get out of London and move to the peace and quiet of the Welsh countryside.

From the moment I sowed my first seeds in my very own garden – soil stuck under my nails – I was hooked. As the roots of those early plants grew, my own roots grew stronger. I felt this overwhelming connection to the land and the earth. The first thing I ever harvested was some simple radishes, and I still remember the peppery taste to this day. With that first bite of a little homegrown radish, still with dirt on the skin, I realized I had never had a vegetable so fresh before. It dawned on me that up until that moment, I'd never really had a connection to where my food came from. After that first harvest, I understood the time, care and dedication that goes into producing food. But more importantly the superiority of *flavour* of homegrown organic produce.

I knew from that moment forward my cooking style would be transformed and it became my mission to encourage my audience to grow their own food and allow their produce to take centre-stage on the plate.

So, welcome to *Plant to Plate*. This book showcases ten of the ingredients I most enjoy growing in my little Welsh homestead and how to best preserve, cook and elevate them to be the main focus on any plate.

As this book is all about plants, the recipes contain zero animal products. They're what I call 'plant forward'. You can, of course, serve the dishes or components with whatever you see fit or usually eat – all I ask is that you perhaps make them as intended the first time you cook them, so you can properly appreciate the power of plants. After growing my own food for four years, I've realized how abundant growing-your-own actually is and the importance of prolonging the freshness of my harvests, so I quickly learned how to preserve my bounty. Within each chapter, you'll find recipes for drying, fermenting and delicious condiments.

It may sound unusual to anyone who isn't a chef, cook or recipe writer, but recipes aren't just a guide on how to make a dish. They're actually more like extensions of our personalities. They are memories of times gone by, influenced by travels to new shores or dinners over the years with loved ones. They are developed with the hope that the feelings and thoughts that went into creating them can transfer to the person who recreates the dish. I hope you experience even a small part of my enthusiasm and passion when making these recipes in your own home.

Respect

If you'd told me five or six years ago that I'd cherish a courgette or pumpkin the way I do today, I'd have thought you'd gone mad. I love it when I see memes that say something like, 'I used to be cool and trendy; now I take photos of my homegrown vegetables.' Nothing could be truer for me. Although, honestly, I think growing food is probably the coolest thing anyone can do.

I love that growing my own food saves me money and means not having to constantly visit the supermarket. But, on a deeper level, I think growing food is kind of revolutionary. Growers, farmers and homesteaders are like rockstars in my eyes and, these days, the heroes I look up to are gardeners. There are too many to name but, over the past few years, I've been lucky enough to meet some of the people who first inspired me to grow my own food, and who I've learned so much from: Charles Dowding, Mothin Ali, Gonzalo Samaranch, Huw Richards, Resh Gala, Siloe Oliveira, Adam Jones, Alessandro Vitale, Jacks Patch, Ben Vanheems, Poppy Okotcha, and many more. They've influenced me beyond words.

One of the best days of my life was visiting Gonzalo's farm, Mestiza de Indias, deep in Mexico's Yucatán. I'd only been growing for a year at that point, and I thought I knew a thing or two. But after that visit, I realized how much bigger the act of growing food really is. Growing has the power to connect us to the natural world on a deeper, more spiritual level. It empowers us to know that we're in control of our destiny, free from dependence on outside systems. It nourishes us with natural, organic foods the way they were meant to be before industrial farming took over. It teaches us patience, nurture and love. Gonzalo spoke about how past generations of Mayan people were exceptional farmers, cultivating food in unique ways that helped their communities thrive. He's made it his mission to teach his local community the traditional ways on his farm, honouring Mayan heritage and uplifting the community. Tasting the produce that day felt like hearing a thousand stories: every bite of tomato, carrot and pepper kissed by the Mexican sun was a reminder that I also wanted to encourage as many people as possible to become a little more self-sufficient, a movement that Gonzalo calls 'a silent revolution'.

Growing my own food isn't just a fun hobby for me. It's all the reasons listed above, but it also supports my mind. My mental health is so much better these days. My garden is like an emotional support system – it's always there with a job to do, giving me purpose whenever I need it. In a world where so many of us are struggling mentally, a garden can be a true sanctuary. Time spent growing food or simply being in nature should be encouraged and taught everywhere because it really is that impactful.

Often, I wish I could talk to my younger self, the one that was ignorant to the efforts that went into growing the ingredients that were delivered to the restaurants he worked in; the one who, only a few years ago, was filling his trolley with tasteless and pesticide-laden strawberries in the middle of winter. Of course, I understand that industrial farming sustains a growing population, but at what cost? Growing our own food shouldn't be a privilege – it never used to be. My granddad grew food in his back garden for my mum when she was young to save costs, and I'm sure the generations before him did the same thing. But now, especially here in the UK, it feels like a lost tradition. What I can do is look forward though, and I'm excited to grow older and wiser as I continue learning about our connection to food and nature and sharing that knowledge with others.

If you've bought this book, I'm guessing you like food as much as I do. You might even already grow some of your own. If that's the case, then you've already likely noticed the difference in taste between organic, good-quality produce and store-bought produce. So, with that in mind, please do me one favour when recreating the recipes in this book. Make sure the star ingredients are in season and homegrown or, if not homegrown, at least sourced from friends' allotments, or a local organic farmers market, or is at the very least organic supermarket produce. Treat these ingredients with the respect they deserve and, I promise, your taste buds and body will thank you for it!

RESPECT

Free Food

After leaving the city and reconnecting with nature through my vegetable garden, the natural next step was to elevate my foraging skills. Over the years, I've gathered wild garlic, berries, gorse and other plants and vegetables. But now, living immersed in the countryside, foraging has become an even bigger part of my life, and I've started foraging not just for food but also for medicinal plants.

As I continue to explore, I feel inspired to fill a whole book with insights on foraging. However, in this book, you'll find just a few of my favourite foraged ingredients, like wild garlic, nettles and blackberries. Although using foraged ingredients might seem intimidating, I hope you'll feel inspired to gain the confidence needed to forage some of your own food (and you can always substitute any foraged ingredients for something else, if you'd prefer). By picking delicious free food, that our ancestors survived on, I hope that you'll instantly feel a connection to nature, just like I do.

With each plant you learn to identify and harvest, you'll develop a deeper understanding of the land and gain a wealth of knowledge about the natural foods available to us throughout the seasons. Foraging is both rewarding and empowering and is a skill that brings us closer to our surroundings. Let's make an effort to reclaim this knowledge of the natural world and pass it on before it fades away for good. I recommend the following books on foraging to help you get started: *The Forager's Calendar* by John Wright, *The Hedgerow Handbook* by Adele Nozedar and *Mushrooms* by Roger Phillips.

Please always forage responsibly, identify plants with certainty, and avoid harvesting in built-up or polluted areas. When in doubt, consult a reliable guide or foraging expert for safety.

It's Alive

Fermentation is one of those ancient arts that you might not even realize we rely on daily, but it's behind so many of the flavours and products we love. From the tangy taste of bread, cheese and yogurt to the punchy flavours in beer and wine, or the umami notes of soy sauce, fermentation has been transforming foods for thousands of years. It's a natural process that not only brings out incredible depth and tanginess, but also preserves food in a way that's simple in process but has mighty results.

Growing my own food taught me the importance of fermentation. It's an essential way to preserve my harvests, maintaining and enhancing the produce from my garden and keeping flavours alive throughout the year. Through fermentation, I can still enjoy the taste of my summer tomatoes in the depths of winter. Nothing goes to waste when you know how to ferment.

In each chapter of this book, you'll find one or two fermentation recipes. I don't want you to be afraid of these. The process is simple and fun, plus having a shelf or cabinet full of your fermenting babies makes your home look alive! (If you'll pardon the pun.)

The main fermenting techniques I showcase in this book are inspired by two of the most well-known fermented dishes: sauerkraut and kimchi.

Like some of my favourite dishes, both sauerkraut and kimchi have their roots in the cuisines of South Asia. Sauerkraut is believed to have originated in China over 2,000 years ago, where workers building the Great Wall ate fermented cabbage preserved in rice wine. This method of food preservation made its way to Europe, where it became a staple in German and Eastern European cuisine (sauerkraut literally translates as 'sour cabbage' in German), loved for its tangy crunch and ability to last through harsh winters. Kimchi has been a central part of Korean cuisine for over 3,000 years. Similar to sauerkraut, it's simply a way to preserve vegetables through the cold months; however, kimchi has evolved into a core part of Korean food culture, with countless variations that add depth, spice and tang to humble vegetables.

Both techniques rely on lacto-fermentation, where the beneficial bacteria *Lactobacillus* (found naturally on the skins of organic fruits and vegetables) is encouraged to thrive in an oxygen-free, salted environment. During fermentation, this bacteria breaks down sugars in the food, creating a tangy flavour and an acidic environment that keeps other, more harmful, bacteria out.

I must stress that the ferments in this book aren't authentic to traditional recipes – they're my interpretations using the ingredients I have to hand. Often, it's a case of 'Oh damn, I've got a ton of tomatoes to harvest. Let's quickly ferment them before they go bad.'

Although fermenting fruits and vegetables is ultimately quite a simple process, there are a few things to bear in mind.

FERMENTATION TROUBLESHOOTING GUIDE

PRODUCE

Please only use organic produce. Fruits and vegetables sprayed with pesticides (even after they've been washed) may affect the quality and success of your ferment. Do not scrub the produce too much either – a light rinse is fine – as you want the beneficial bacteria on the skins to stay intact.

EQUIPMENT

A set of digital scales (see below), a large mixing bowl (to combine all your ingredients) and some large jars are all you need to get started. I tend to use a 3-litre (5-pint) jar for my ferments, as it has plenty of space and ensures there is enough empty space at the top of the jar to prevent the brine leaking from the top as it continues to ferment. For smaller quantities, I also use a 2-litre (3½-pint) jar. As you get used to making ferments, you'll better be able to gauge which size of jar you'll need.

STERILIZATION

Clean jars and equipment are essential to prevent unwanted bacteria being introduced to your ferment. You can do this in a few ways:

- Wash and rinse everything thoroughly in warm soapy water.
- Add your jars and equipment to a large saucepan and fill it with water. Bring it to a boil, then turn off the heat and leave everything to cool completely before using.
- Run everything through a hot cycle in your dishwasher.

DIGITAL SCALES

To make any ferment, you need to be able to work out exactly how much salt you need to add to your vegetables. You do this by first weighing all your ingredients, and from there you can calculate the weight of salt you need. It's super important to use accurate digital scales when fermenting, so invest in a decent set! You can buy good-quality digital scales at very affordable prices these days.

SALT PERCENTAGES

Generally speaking, you need to add 2–3% of the weight of vegetables in natural sea salt to create a good environment for lacto-fermentation. I tweak this percentage based on the density of the ingredients I'm using. For example, for something soft and a little watery, like a tomato, I'll stick with 2% salt. For a denser ingredient, like cabbage, I go with 3% salt. Ultimately, it's down to your personal preference.

PACKING THE JAR

Always pack your ingredients as tightly as possible into the jars to reduce air pockets. I use a wooden cocktail muddler for this, but you can use the handle of a wooden spoon. Leave about 5cm (2 inches) of headroom at the top of the jar above whatever you are fermenting.

BRINE COVERAGE

It is essential that your vegetables are always submerged beneath the brine, anything sticking out of the brine or floating on the surface is coming into contact with oxygen and can therefore cause mould to form. To prevent this, I make a 'plug' using something like a cabbage leaf, slice of onion, or a sheet of nori seaweed – anything large enough to hold the other ingredients below the brine.

If you don't have enough brine to cover the mixture, weigh out a little filtered water and then work out what 2–3% of that weight is to give you the weight of salt you need. Whisk the salt into the filtered water until it is completely dissolved, then use this liquid to top up your jar until the mixture is covered.

FERMENTATION WEIGHTS

As well as using a vegetable plug, I recommend investing in glass fermentation weights. These aren't essential, but they do help to keep everything under the brine as they're heavy enough not to float like a vegetable plug often does. I usually do both – I cap my ferment with a vegetable plug then add a sterilized fermentation weight on top – to ensure my ferments never fail.

LABELLING

Always label your ferments and include the start date on your jars so you can track fermentation time. You can also note down the salt percentage, which is helpful for future adjustments.

TEMPERATURES

Fermentation works best at 18–22°C (64–71°F). During winter, my ferments often take twice as long as they do during the summer months to reach a flavour I'm happy with, before I transfer the jar to the fridge. On the other

hand, hot temperatures will speed up the process, so you'll need to keep a close eye on your ferments during the summer.

BURPING JARS

You will need to open your jar every day or two to release the build-up of gases from your ferment (especially during the first few days when fermentation is most active). This prevents pressure building up, which can cause brine to leak out and cause a mess. If you find the brine does leak, that's OK. It just means the jar was slightly overfilled. If necessary, simply pour out a little of the brine and set the jar on a plate to catch any leaks.

WHEN IS IT READY?

Taste your ferment after about a week; when it reaches a deep tangy flavour that you like and it isn't super salty, transfer the jar to the fridge to slow down fermentation.

FRIDGE LIFESPAN

As I mentioned, fermentation gives you the ability to enjoy the flavours of spring and summer in the depths of winter. Once in the fridge, most ferments will keep for months, or even up to a year, depending on the type and salt level. Do be aware that as they continue to ferment, the flavours will deepen further and become even more tangy.

YOUR GUT WILL THANK YOU

Fermentation creates probiotics that can give our gut the love it needs and promote a balanced microbiome, which is essential for digestion and overall well-being.

MOULD

If you see any signs of yeast on the surface of the brine or plug, skim it off immediately and replace the plug. The mixture underneath should still be fine. If you see mould forming, then your ferment has been compromised and you'll likely need to throw it away (into the compost is best!).

Important Equipment

POTS & PANS

I really recommend using stainless steel or cast-iron pans. With a little love and care they should last a lifetime.

GOOD-QUALITY CHOPPING BOARD

Invest in a sturdy wooden chopping board. They look great and will last a lifetime.

GOOD-QUALITY KNIFE

Please invest in a sharp chef's knife. Not only are they safer to use, they will make you more efficient and neater when chopping.

SILICONE SPATULA

My favourite tool in the kitchen – easy to clean and saves on waste.

MANDOLINE

Not essential, but handy when you want really fine slices. Be sure to always use a guard when using a mandoline.

WEIGHING SCALES & CUP MEASURES

I use cup measures for convenience a lot of the time in the kitchen, but electric weighing scales are much more accurate, especially when baking or calculating salt measurements for my ferments, so I recommend having both on hand.

BLENDER & FOOD PROCESSOR

A powerful blender is essential when you want the smoothest of soups or sauces. I recommend a Thermomix or Vitamix. A food processor is also useful for finely chopping lots of ingredients.

MUSLIN / CHEESECLOTH

It's always useful to have a roll of this in your kitchen – I use it to strain things or use it to cover my ferments.

FERMENTATION EQUIPMENT

See page 16.

BBQ OR FIRE PIT

If you have space for a little outdoor kitchen, then invest in a BBQ or fire pit. This is the original way to cook, and with every meal you cook outside you'll feel more connected to the world and our ancestors. I think every vegetable garden should have a fire pit, for spontaneous cook-ups.

Pantry Essentials

A GENERAL NOTE

All ingredients used within this book are free of animal products, but you can adapt them to suit your tastes and needs. For those that follow a plant-forward diet, please be aware that every time I mention pastry, milk, yogurt, butter and ice cream (or any other dairy products), that these are plant-based varieties (and the recipes have been developed and tested as such). For milk I tend to use oat or hemp, and for butter I use an olive oil and shea blend – but simply use what is most convenient for you.

HERBS & SPICES

If you're into cooking, you'll know how the addition of dried herbs and spices can supercharge flavour in your dishes. I recommend buying them in bulk or from zero waste shops and storing them in labelled jars. Better yet, grow and dry your own herbs and spices for an endless supply. Herbs are easy to grow and, when they go to seed, the seeds can be harvested and then sown to grow more herbs next year, or turned into dried spices. I have herbs hanging upside down in my kitchen drying out all year round – as soon as they're dry, I blitz them to a powder and store them in jars.

SEA SALT

Natural sea salt is an absolute must and, if it's local, then all the better. I use a Welsh sea salt called Halen Môn from Anglesey, North Wales. When making ferments it's even more important to use good-quality sea salt: never use table salt.

COOKING OILS

I often get asked what oils I cook with. For frying, I tend to use avocado oil or cold-pressed rapeseed (canola) oil, which is local to me. For dressings, I use good-quality extra virgin olive oil.

MISO

By far the most important ingredient in my pantry, miso is a fermented and aged Japanese paste made from beans (such as soy), sea salt and koji (a type of mould starter combined with rice or barley). The paste is fermented for months or sometimes years to develop a rich, savoury, umami flavour that is packed with gut-friendly bacteria. I now make my own miso

and I refer to the jar as my miso baby because it takes nine months to ferment! Nowadays, you can get good-quality miso from all large supermarkets. I add it to an array of dishes in this book to add depth and complexity.

SOY SAUCE & TAMARI

An absolute essential in a plant-forward kitchen, just like miso, soy sauce and tamari both add depth and an almost meaty flavour to dishes. Tamari is a gluten-free version of soy sauce and is actually a by-product of making miso, so I often harvest my own while my miso is aging.

NORI OR OTHER DRIED SEAWEED

I always have dried seaweed on hand to add depth and a taste of the sea to sauces and stews. I also use sheets of nori to plug many of my ferments (page 16).

DRIED BEANS & GRAINS

My kitchen is filled with jars of dried beans (some homegrown) and grains. I buy both in bulk to save on cost and to reduce packaging. I find beans and grains cooked from dry taste so much better than their canned/jarred equivalents. Yes, you have to soak the beans overnight and cook them for an hour or so, but the end result is worth it. All of the recipes in this book that require beans or grains can be cooked with both dried and canned varieties, but this is my little request that you start using dried.

DRIED MUSHROOMS

As important to me as miso, dried mushrooms are a trick up your sleeve if you want to add punch to a dish. The drying process intensifies their flavour, meaning that you don't need many to transform a recipe. Ensure your pantry is stocked with a couple of varieties – my favourites are porcini and shiitake.

NUTS & SEEDS

I rely heavily on the nutrients nuts and seeds offer, and my kitchen is lined with jars of them – from hemp and chia seeds, to macadamia nuts. Not only are they good for you, they add complex and delicious flavours to many of the dishes in this book. So head down to your local zero waste shop and stock up. They'll sustain you when you most need it and elevate your food in the process.

FLOURS

In this book I use a variety of flours (rye, spelt, double zero, self raising, plain/all-purpose, cornflour/cornstarch). Experimenting with different or ancient grains will add a twist to your food.

SWEETENERS

In this book I rely on natural sweeteners like dried fruit, dates, coconut sugar, date sugar and maple syrup. I really try to avoid refined sugar as much as I can, so have a go at swapping them out with the more natural sweeteners – you'll be surprised at the flavour profile they add to recipes.

Star Ingredients

Let's talk about the star ingredients I focus on in this book. I've chosen ten easily accessible ingredients that we know and love – all of which I grow in my garden. These ten ingredients are fairly easy to grow and are staples in my kitchen. In each chapter, I'll show you how to preserve, elevate and enhance their flavour.

STRAWBERRY

Strawberries signify summer for me, and their flavour is unbeatable. They spread and grow like weeds if not contained – in fact, many gardeners might get mad at me for how I let my strawberries wander and take over my garden paths. I love it though – the more strawberries, the better! If I had to choose only one crop each year, it would be strawberries. About 75% never make it to the kitchen, because I simply enjoy them as I stroll barefoot around the garden in summer. Check out the strawberry chapter for recipes showcasing the ones that do make it to the kitchen.

POTATO

I have a feeling this chapter will be the most loved and used. We all adore potatoes – I could write an entire book on them! There are over 4,000 varieties of potatoes in the world. In Peru, where potatoes originated, specific dishes call for specific varieties. It's definitely a place I'd love to visit – potato heaven! I grow a lot of potatoes; they're easy to grow and an essential crop. They store for months, providing food year-round. If you want to try growing potatoes, grab some large buckets, fill them with rich compost, and drop 2–3 potatoes in, about halfway down. Before long, you'll have a bounty of new potatoes!

CARROT

Out of the all the many ingredients I grow at home, the taste difference is most noticeable between my homegrown carrots and those from the supermarket. Homegrown carrots are crisper, juicier and sweeter. It's like a lucky dip when I pull up my carrots; sometimes they're big, sometimes tiny and sometimes a little x-rated in shape – but that's the fun of homegrown!

COURGETTE

I honestly think that courgettes are the crop that, per plant, pump out the most amount of food. You're sometimes overrun with them and, if you forget about them, suddenly they've turned into giant marrows. If I ever have a glut, I whip up my courgette kimchi (page 98) or make a batch of cookies (page 103). If you're a newbie to growing food, you can't go wrong with growing courgettes! Pick them when they're small for a sweeter more vibrant flavour and don't forget to make use of their delicious flowers.

TOMATO

I devote the majority of my greenhouse to my beloved tomatoes. Next to each vine, I plant a small basil companion plant. Just as they pair perfectly on the plate, they complement each other in the garden. Most of the tomatoes I grow are preserved. When I mention preservation, most people assume I turn them into sauce. But actually, I make loads of tomato kimchi (page 122). Try it – I promise your taste buds will be amazed.

BEETROOT

Convincing people to enjoy beetroot can be challenging; its earthy flavour isn't for everyone. But when homegrown and cooked right, it's a joy for the palate. I think beetroots are wonders of the garden. While they may look dirty and unexciting at first, slicing into them reveals a spectacular array of colours, from pink-and-white striped, deep purples, reds and even golden yellows. I grow a variety of beetroots, and they can be transformed into decadent dishes and even desserts!

CHILLI

I sow my chilli seeds in the middle of January, indoors on heat mats under lights. This is the commitment needed to grow chillies in a cold country like Wales! But the investment is more than worth it. I try to grow a few different varieties, but my all-time favourite is scotch bonnets, which feature heavily in this chapter. They have the most flavour as well as a fiery kick. Feel free to use whatever chillies you prefer or grow for any of the recipes in the chilli chapter.

ONION

I try to grow enough onions to last the whole year – they can last about ten months if stored correctly. After harvesting, I let them dry and then braid the stalks, hanging them as decorations in my kitchen until I need them (having my homegrown harvests decorate my house has always been a dream of mine). The onion chapter might be my favourite, and my stuffed onion recipe (page 198) is always a hit with friends and family. Onions are relatively easy to grow and pair well with carrots, as they help deter each other's pests.

APPLE

They say that future generations will reap the benefits of fruit trees planted today, and that certainly is true for the apple and other fruit trees I planted when I first moved to my homestead four years ago. So far I've only harvested about 30 apples, but each year brings more. Fortunately, my neighbour has prolific, mature apple trees, and many locals often have tons of apples they're desperate to share. Apples are humble and underrated, so I make sure to elevate them in this chapter with unique and delicious recipes.

PUMPKIN & SQUASH

Each year, my pumpkins grow bigger and better! Soon, I might be able to carve a door and move into one! A pumpkin patch adds a whimsical touch to a cottage garden, with vines trailing everywhere and vibrant fruits (appearing as if by magic) that can be used to make elegant dishes. The seeds provide a secondary harvest that I use in various recipes, from homemade ferments (page 228) to nutritious bars (page 235).

strawberry

Baked Strawberry, Watermelon & Pistachio Salad

SERVES 4

1 small red onion,
roughly chopped

3 garlic cloves, peeled

Thumb-sized piece of ginger,
peeled and roughly chopped

3 tbsp pistachio butter or tahini

1 tbsp za'atar spice blend

2 tsp miso paste

Handful of curly parsley,
plus extra to finish

3 tbsp coconut sugar

2 tsp dried chilli flakes
(red pepper flakes)

3 tbsp white wine vinegar

300g (10½oz) watermelon, peeled

300g (10½oz) strawberries,
green tops removed and halved

300g (2 cups/10½oz) giant
(pearl) couscous

200g (7oz) green tomatoes,
cut into chunks

4 tbsp extra virgin olive oil

45g (⅓ cup/1½oz) toasted
pistachio nuts

To serve (optional)

Fresh herbs

Hummus

A savoury strawberry dish that uses some of my favourite flavours from across the world. Za'atar originated in the area of the Middle East where modern-day Syria, Lebanon, Palestine and Jordan are located. It is one of the oldest spice blends on the planet – a beautiful blend typically containing wild thyme, sumac, sesame, oregano and salt. If you can't find za'atar pre-mixed, then just blend equal quantities of the forementioned ingredients.

Baking strawberries concentrates their flavour, and the watermelon transforms into the most unique divine texture. It's all served and mopped up with giant couscous, but any grain of your choice will work with this dish. My homegrown green tomatoes add a touch of freshness that I love, but you can use any tomatoes you have to hand.

Preheat your oven to 180°C/160°C fan (350°F/Gas Mark 4).

Add the onion, garlic, ginger, pistachio butter or tahini, za'atar, miso, parsley, sugar, chilli flakes and vinegar to a food processor and blitz to a smooth paste.

Cut the watermelon into cubes and add to a roasting tray with the halved strawberries and blended paste. Mix really well, then bake in the oven for 1 hour.

Meanwhile, cook your couscous according to the packet instructions.

When the watermelon is completely tender, remove the tray from the oven and allow to cool slightly.

Stir the green tomatoes, olive oil, some extra parsley and the pistachios through the giant couscous. Serve up the baked strawberries and watermelon on top of a bed of couscous and drizzle any baking juices all around the plate. I serve mine with fresh herbs and my burnt onion hummus (see page 186).

Cardamom & Balsamic Strawberries with Fire Bread

A campfire dish that is filled with whimsy – there's something magical about cooking blind using a Dutch oven pot. You have to trust your instinct and be brave, as cooking over fire involves all your senses. You'll start to smell the sweet strawberries and roasting bread when it's almost ready, and, hey, if it's a little charred in parts, it just adds to the charm. Of course, this dish can also be baked in a conventional oven at 220°C/200°C fan (425°F/Gas Mark 7), for 25–30 minutes.

SERVES 6

For the bread dough

350ml (1½ cups) warm water

4 tbsp maple syrup

1 tsp dried fast action yeast

½ tsp ground cardamom

4 tbsp sesame seeds

Pinch of sea salt

4 tbsp extra virgin olive oil, plus extra for greasing

425g (3 cups/15oz) strong white bread flour

For the strawberries

300g (10½oz) strawberries, halved

5 tbsp maple syrup

4 tbsp balsamic vinegar

Pinch of ground cardamom

3 tbsp olive oil

Handful of mint leaves, plus extra to serve

To serve

Ice cream (see page 140 for homemade)

Tahini

Maple syrup

Toasted sesame seeds

First, prep the bread dough. Whisk the water, maple syrup, yeast, cardamom, sesame seeds, salt and oil together in a large bowl, then fold through the flour. Stir really well until combined, making sure the dough is super smooth. Cover the bowl and place somewhere warm for 3 hours.

Meanwhile, in another bowl, mix together the strawberries, maple syrup, vinegar, cardamom, olive oil and mint. Set this aside too.

About 30 minutes before the dough is ready, light your fire and make sure you have plenty of hot white coals.

When the dough has risen, grease a large 23cm (9-inch) cast-iron Dutch oven pot with a little oil. Carefully transfer the dough to the pot, avoiding bursting the light, airy bubbles. Top it with the strawberry mixture and place the lid on the pot.

Clear a space in the coals for the pot to sit (you don't want the pot to sit directly on the coals, otherwise the bottom of the bread will burn), then place the pot in the fire. Use tongs to arrange coals around the sides and on top of the pot.

Leave the bread to bake for 35–50 minutes, occasionally rotating the pot and starting to check after 30 minutes to see if it's cooked. It's rather subjective, but for me if it's golden, caramelized and bubbly, it's ready.

Serve up directly from the pan, with ice cream, tahini, maple syrup, toasted sesame seeds and fresh mint.

Fermented Strawberries with Whipped Macadamia Nut Yogurt

Strawberries are an excellent fruit for lacto-fermentation, as their natural sweetness transforms into a beautiful balance of tangy and savoury flavours during the process. It's a delicious way to enjoy them, and preserves your harvest for months to come.

Paired with the creamy nuttiness of my macadamia nut yogurt, this simple dish nonetheless offers a complex taste. It's perfect for a late-summer weekend breakfast.

SERVES 2-4

500g (1lb 2oz) strawberries, green tops removed and halved

10g (¼oz) sea salt

For the dressing

3 tbsp ferment brine (from the strawberries)

3 tbsp maple syrup

2 tbsp poppy seeds

3 tbsp basil leaves, ideally Greek, finely chopped

For the whipped yogurt

220g (1 cup/7¾oz) coconut yogurt

5 tbsp macadamia nut butter

Zest and juice of 1 lemon

To garnish and serve

Toasted macadamia nuts

Sourdough bread

Place the strawberries in a bowl and sprinkle over the salt. Stir really well, then cover the bowl with a clean tea (dish) towel and let the strawberries sit at room temperature for about 3 hours. The salt will naturally draw out the liquid from the strawberries, creating a brine that they will then ferment in.

When the brine created is visible, transfer the strawberries and brine to a sterilized jar and hold everything beneath the brine with a fermentation weight. Make sure you've added enough brine to cover the mixture by around 1cm (½ inch) (see page 15 for my fermentation troubleshooting guide). Be sure to leave about 2.5cm (1 inch) of headroom at the top of the jar, then seal the lid.

Place your jar somewhere warm to ferment for 4–5 days, and 'burp' the jar every now and then, to release any build-up of gas (see page 17 for my fermentation troubleshooting guide). When the brine tastes tangy, the strawberries are ready. You can serve them straight away or place the jar in the fridge, where fermentation will slow down and the strawberries will last for months.

When ready to serve, combine all the dressing ingredients.

Whisk the coconut yogurt, macadamia nut butter and lemon zest and juice together in a bowl, mixing until really light and creamy.

Spread a spoonful of the whipped macadamia nut yogurt onto a plate, top with some fermented strawberries and drizzle with the dressing. Garnish with toasted macadamia nuts and serve with toasted sourdough.

Strawberry & Lavender Welsh Cakes

These little cakes are a classic from my homeland of Wales, and I would describe them as a blend between a scone (biscuit) and a pancake. Traditionally, they're made with currants, but here I've used my homegrown dried strawberries and lavender.

MAKES ABOUT 16

250g (1¾ cups/9oz) plain (all-purpose) flour, plus extra for dusting

100g (½ cup/3½oz) caster (superfine) sugar, plus extra to serve

75g (⅔ cup/2½oz) dried strawberries (see below)

1 tsp baking powder

½ tsp bicarbonate of soda (baking soda)

½ tsp ground cinnamon

½ tsp ground nutmeg

½ tsp ground ginger

2 tbsp dried lavender flowers

Pinch of sea salt

125g (½ cup/4½oz) cold butter, cubed

About 5 tbsp cold milk

Oil, for greasing

For the dried strawberries (makes about 50g/1¾oz)

500g (1lb 2oz) strawberries, green tops removed

Add all the dry ingredients to a large bowl and mix thoroughly. Add the butter and rub it into the flour mixture with your fingers until it forms a breadcrumb-like consistency.

Stir in enough milk to bind the mixture into a dough. Tip the dough out onto a floured surface and roll to the thickness of your little finger. Using a 5cm (2-inch) cookie cutter, cut the dough into discs.

Preheat a heavy-based skillet over a low heat. Rub a tiny bit of oil in the pan, then cook the Welsh cakes, in batches, for about 4 minutes on each side, until golden.

Generously sprinkle over some sugar to serve, and enjoy them while still warm for the best Welsh cake experience.

DRIED STRAWBERRIES

I love dried strawberries as a snack or as topping on my daily oatmeal – another great way to preserve the harvest for ages!

Slice the strawberries 2mm (¹⁄₁₆ inch) thick and lay them on your dehydrator sheets. Set the temperature of your dehydrator to 40°C (104°F) and dry for 24 hours or until fully crisp.

You can also use your oven for this; just set it to 90°C (200°F/Gas Mark ¼) and lay the strawberry slices out on baking parchment, then bake until completely dry, around 4 hours.

Strawberry Jerk Oyster Mushrooms with Strawberry Scotch Bonnet Dressing

SERVES 4

4 oyster mushroom clusters or 10 large portobello mushrooms

4 tbsp olive oil

For the strawberry jerk sauce

6 spring onions (scallions), roughly chopped

5 garlic cloves, peeled

½ Scotch bonnet chilli

100g (3½oz) strawberries

4 tbsp soy sauce or coconut aminos

3 tbsp thyme leaves

2 tsp ground allspice

1 tbsp minced fresh ginger

2 tbsp coconut sugar

1 tsp ground cinnamon

1 tsp ground nutmeg

1 tbsp tomato paste

½ tsp sea salt

To serve

Rice

Roasted cashew nuts

Sautéed greens

Jerk cooking has a special place in my heart, and so does Jamaica. Many of the best times of my life have been on that beautiful island – the rich culture, rhythm and mystical feeling that I experience there is something I've not felt elsewhere. For the rest of my life, Jamaica will always call me and I'll always be inspired by the cuisine; in fact, I now grow tons of spring onions, thyme and scotchies (aka Scotch bonnets), all of which are essential in jerk and Jamaican cuisine in general.

Jerk originated with the indigenous Taíno tribes of the island, and was carried forward by the Jamaican Maroons who connected with the tribes in the 17th century. The Maroons were Africans who broke free from enslavement and took refuge in the mountains, forging self-sufficient communities and connecting deeply with the land. The jerk-marinated meats were often cooked slowly in underground oven pits to minimize the smoke, so as not to give their locations away. It was also a technique used to preserve meat. Jerk is more than just a dish, it's a sign of resilience, and holds a poignant story of Jamaica's history.

Cooking jerk with my friend, chef Vita, up in the Blue Mountains was a moment I will never forget, and when I got back to my homestead in Wales, upon harvesting tons of sweet strawberries, I thought, why not replace the sweet elements that are often added to jerk pastes with my strawberries? It worked a treat, so this dish is my adaptation of jerk, using homegrown strawberries, spring onions, Scotch bonnet, garlic and thyme. Just like chef Vita and I cooked up in the hills, I use mushrooms for the meaty element. Rastafarians do not eat meat, but the texture of mushrooms gives you everything you need for when it comes to 'meaty' jerk.

Preheat your oven to 220°C/200°C fan (425°F/Gas Mark 7).

Add all the jerk sauce ingredients to a food processor and blitz into a paste. Check for seasoning and spice, then set aside.

Trim any tough parts from the base of the oyster mushroom clusters, halving any that are very large (if using portobello mushrooms, simply score them with a sharp knife). Place an ovenproof pan (ideally cast iron) over a high heat and add the olive oil. When hot, sear the mushrooms for around 5 minutes on each side, using a press, the base of another heavy pan, or wooden spatula to press the mushrooms as they cook, helping them to release any liquid and achieve a meaty texture.

Continued...

Once caramelized, flip and cook them until caramelized on the other side. When the mushrooms are golden, begin brushing them with lashings of the jerk sauce, using a pastry brush or rosemary sprig to apply it.

Flip, baste and cook until the mushrooms are really sticky and caramelized, then add a bit more jerk sauce (reserving a little for later) and place the pan in the hot oven for 10–15 minutes, to allow the mushrooms to char a little and get even more tender.

Serve the mushrooms up with some rice, roasted cashews, sautéed greens and any remaining jerk sauce.

Note
You can also cook and baste the mushrooms on the BBQ until sticky, charred and tender.

Strawberry & Hibiscus Chutney

If you're wondering what to do with a bounty of homegrown strawberries, turning them into a tangy, sweet and savoury chutney is a fantastic way to preserve their flavour and create a versatile condiment you'll want to use on everything. My addition of hibiscus is inspired by a trip to my friend Marianna's restaurant in Kingston, Jamaica. Though her restaurant is no longer there, it was a huge success, blending the flavours of her Middle Eastern heritage with Jamaica's vibrant produce. One standout dish was her hibiscus (also known as sorrel) chutney, served with cornbread. I love adding dried hibiscus to my strawberry chutney for its sour, fruity tang and the deep colour it imparts. Hibiscus is uplifting and also makes a delightful tea, so I always keep it stocked in my pantry. When rehydrated, the flowers have a satisfying bite that gives this strawberry chutney extra texture and depth.

FILLS A 1-LITRE (2-PINT) JAR

5 tbsp dried hibiscus

1kg (2lb 3oz) strawberries, green tops removed and quartered

1 tbsp minced fresh ginger

1 red onion, finely chopped

1 red chilli, finely chopped

125ml (½ cup) white wine vinegar

200g (1 cup/7oz) caster (superfine) or coconut sugar

1 tsp ground allspice

2 cloves

½ tsp sea salt

Roughly chop the dried hibiscus into smaller pieces, then add it to a large, heavy-based saucepan with the remaining ingredients and stir well. Place over a very low heat and let the mixture bubble away for 90 minutes, stirring often.

After 90 minutes the strawberries should have broken down and the liquid should be jammy. To test if it is ready, dip a spoon in the chutney; if it leaves a glossy, sticky residue on the spoon, and after wiping your finger across it the glaze clings and holds, it's a sign that it's done.

Transfer the chutney to a sterilized jar while still hot. When cooled, transfer to the fridge, where it will keep for up to 3 months.

Strawberry Kombucha

Kombucha is so good for you – this one tastes like summer and is the perfect refreshment after a day outside or a workout at the end of the day. If you need any additional guidance, or want to experiment with kombucha, I have a whole kombucha masterclass episode on my YouTube channel. You can use the base kombucha recipe to infuse with any flavour your mind can imagine. Some of my favourites are rhubarb and rose, blackberry and mint, and hibiscus and ginger.

MAKES 5-10 BOTTLES

4 litres (4¼ quarts) filtered water

8 black tea bags (I use Assam)

200g (1 cup/7oz) raw cane sugar

500ml (2 cups) kombucha starter (pre-made natural kombucha)

1 large SCOBY (Symbiotic Culture of Bacteria and Yeast)

200g (7oz) organic strawberries, green tops removed and halved

Equipment

5-litre (5¼-quart) glass fermentation jar with a tap (wide-mouthed works best), sterilized

Cheesecloth

Elastic band or string

Funnel, sterilized

Either five 1-litre (2-pint) or ten 500-ml (1-pint) glass bottles with lids, sterilized

Begin by boiling the filtered water in a large saucepan. Once it's at a rolling boil, remove from the heat, add the tea and steep for 10 minutes, then remove the bags. Add the sugar and mix to dissolve fully. Allow to cool to room temperature.

Pass the cooled tea through a sieve (strainer) into your fermentation jar. Stir the kombucha starter through the cooled tea, using a wooden spoon. Place the SCOBY in the jar, then cover the jar with a piece of cheesecloth and secure with an elastic band or string.

Place the jar in a warm, dark place for about 7–14 days. The fermentation time can vary depending on the temperature and how tart you like your kombucha. During this time, the SCOBY will consume the sugar, creating a fizzy, tangy tea full of beneficial bacteria. If the kombucha is very sweet still and there's no sign of a new layer of SCOBY formed, then give it more time – a warmer environment will accelerate this process. Sometimes, in winter, my kombucha needs to ferment for up to 3 weeks. Once it's fizzy and tastes to your liking, it's ready for bottling.

Blitz the strawberries to a purée in a food processor, then pass through a fine sieve to remove any seeds. (Alternatively, you can just add small chunks of strawberry directly to the bottles.)

Add a few tablespoons of the strawberry purée to the bottom of each bottle, then use a funnel to fill your bottles with kombucha, leaving at least 2.5cm (1 inch) of headroom. Make sure you leave at least 500ml (2 cups) of the kombucha in the fermentation jar to kickstart your next batch. Seal the bottles tight.

Leave the bottles to ferment out of the fridge for a further 2–3 days before placing them in the fridge, where fermentation will slow down and they will keep for up to 6 months.

Note
The bottles you use need to be able to withstand pressure so that they don't explode. Clean screw-top wine bottles will work, as will swing-top glass bottles (which is what I prefer to use).

Strawberry Sorbet with Strawberry Top & Dill Oil

Simple strawberry sorbet using no refined sugars, with the maple adding a subtle spiced flavour. This sorbet is elevated by the herbaceous oil made from often discarded strawberry tops and dill. Strawberry tops are actually rich in antioxidants, and I'm one of those strange people who always eats the greens along with the strawberries, for all their goodness. You can use the oil in salad dressings too, or to drizzle on savoury dishes.

MAKES JUST OVER 1 LITRE (2 PINTS)

900g (2lb) strawberries, green tops removed but reserved

180ml (¾ cup) maple syrup

125ml (½ cup) water

Juice of ½ lemon

2 tbsp vanilla bean paste

For the strawberry top and dill oil

20g (1 cup/¾oz) dill, including stalks, plus a few leaves to garnish

Green strawberry tops (taken from 900g/2lb strawberries; see above)

180ml (¾ cup) flavourless oil, such as cold-pressed rapeseed (canola) oil

Add about 90% of the strawberries to a blender and blitz until super smooth. Finely chop the remaining strawberries and set aside. Pass the blitzed strawberry purée through a fine sieve (strainer) into a bowl, then stir through the chopped strawberries, maple syrup, water, lemon juice and vanilla. Taste for sweetness, then transfer to your ice-cream machine and let the machine work its magic.

If not using a machine, simply transfer the sorbet mixture to a bowl or tub in your freezer. After 30 minutes, vigorously hand-mix the mixture with a fork or whisk – do this every 30 minutes until it is totally set.

Transfer the frozen sorbet to a tub or container and place in your freezer, where it can store for months. I recommend removing it from the freezer 15 minutes before enjoying, to make it easier to scoop.

To serve, make your dill oil. Blitz the dill, including the stalks, with the reserved strawberry tops and oil until smooth. Pass the mixture through a fine sieve or cheesecloth. After straining you'll be left with a super-green oil; it will be slightly grassy, bitter and herbaceous, which will complement the strawberry sorbet really well.

This oil can be stored in the fridge for a few weeks and used to bring life to other dishes.

Garnish the sorbet with a drizzle of strawberry top and dill oil, and a few dill leaves.

potato

Chard Aloo

If you have a vegetable garden, you'll know how abundant Swiss chard is, and I'm forever thinking of ways how to enjoy it. It's actually one of my favourite ingredients, and it works brilliantly instead of spinach in this re-imagined classic north Indian dish (saag aloo), especially if you're using homegrown spuds.

SERVES 4

3 tbsp olive oil

1 tsp mustard seeds

½ tsp ground turmeric

1 tsp fennel seeds

1 tbsp minced fresh ginger

6 garlic cloves, minced

1 hot red chilli, finely sliced

½ tsp ground fenugreek

½ tsp ground cumin

2 large tomatoes, diced

1 tsp sea salt

4 medium potatoes, cubed

250ml (1 cup) vegetable stock

2 big handfuls of chard
(or spinach), stalks and
leaves finely shredded

1 tbsp garam masala

For the dressing

120ml (½ cup) olive oil

Handful of coriander (cilantro)

Zest and juice of 1 lemon

5 tbsp hemp seeds

2 garlic cloves, minced

1 tsp garam masala

Pinch of sea salt

1 green chilli

Heat the olive oil in a large pan over a medium heat. Add the mustard seeds and allow them to sizzle and pop, then stir in the turmeric and fennel seeds. After a few moments, add the ginger, garlic and chilli, stirring them into the oil until fragrant.

Cook for a couple of minutes, then stir in the ground fenugreek and cumin. Cook for 30 more seconds, then add the tomatoes and salt and allow the tomatoes to soften and cook down, creating a bit of a sauce.

Add the potatoes, then deglaze the pan with the stock. Cover and let the potatoes cook away until just cooked through.

Add the shredded chard and garam masala and stir them through the potatoes. Place the lid back on the pan, turn the heat down to low and let the chard cook down for 3–4 minutes.

Meanwhile, add all the dressing ingredients to a small food processor and blitz to create a little vibrant dressing.

Spoon the dressing over the chard aloo just before serving.

Fluffy Spelt Potato Bread

*Adding potato to bread creates a softer, fluffier loaf. I pair it with spelt,
which is an ancient grain readily available at most supermarkets that has
a nutty flavour I really enjoy. The addition of fennel seeds brings a surprise
to the palate and adds a little sparkle to a very humble bread recipe.
Feel free to get creative and add flavourings of your choice.*

*I will often cook my potatoes for the mash on the fire – the smokiness
transfers through to the bread – but it's not essential; as long as you have
a lovely, smooth mash, then you'll be fine.*

**MAKES 2 X 900G
(2LB) LOAVES**

360ml (1½ cups) warm water
(use the potato cooking water
if boiling them)

3 tbsp maple syrup

4 tbsp extra virgin olive oil,
plus extra for greasing

1 tbsp dried fast action yeast

480g (2 cups/1lb 1oz) mashed
potatoes (see page 61 for
guidance)

700g (5 cups/25oz) spelt flour,
plus extra for dusting

2 tsp fine sea salt

2 tsp fennel seeds (optional)

In a large bowl, mix the water, maple syrup and olive oil. Whisk in
the yeast, then let it sit for a few minutes until the mixture becomes
slightly frothy. Once the yeast has come alive, stir in the mashed
potatoes and mix really well.

Add the flour, salt and fennel seeds, if using, then start to mix
together with a spatula until a dough comes together. Turn the
dough out onto a lightly floured surface and knead for around
5–6 minutes until smooth and elastic; try to resist adding extra flour
as this will make the bread dense. The more you knead the dough,
the less sticky it'll become as the proteins in the flour are activated.

Place the dough in an oiled bowl and cover with a damp cloth.
Place somewhere warm to rise until it has doubled in size; this
should take around 2 hours.

Once the dough has risen, knock it back, then turn it out onto the
work surface and divide it into two equal portions. Shape each
piece into a loaf shape, then place them into lightly greased 900g
(2lb) loaf tins. Let the dough rise again somewhere warm until it
has expanded to fill the tins and risen considerably, about 1 hour.

Preheat your oven to 220°C/200°C fan (425°F/Gas Mark 7). Dust
the risen loaves with a sprinkling of flour and bake in the hot oven
for 35–40 minutes, until golden brown.

Remove from the oven and let the loaves cool on a wire rack
before slicing.

Hummus & Spinach Mashed Potato with Black Beans

All my favourite things on one plate – hummus, spinach, potato – served with Cuban-style black beans! Comfort food at its finest.

SERVES 4

For the black beans

550g (3 cups/1lb 3½oz) dried black beans, soaked overnight

1.5 litres (6 cups) vegetable stock

5 spring onions (scallions), finely chopped

6 garlic cloves, finely chopped

2 tsp ground cumin

1 tbsp dried oregano

1 tbsp dried thyme leaves

2 bay leaves

2 tsp celery salt

2 dried chillies, such as ancho and pasilla (optional)

3 tbsp white wine vinegar

3 tbsp soy sauce

2 tbsp miso paste

6g (½ cup/¼oz) dried mushrooms

For the mashed potato

4 large Maris Piper potatoes, peeled and cubed

240ml (1 cup) milk

½ onion

3 garlic cloves, peeled

1 bay leaf

1 tsp sea salt

1 tsp ground white pepper

150g (½ cup/5½oz) good-quality hummus

5 tbsp extra virgin olive oil

200g (7oz) baby spinach leaves, steamed

Drain and rinse the beans, then add them to a large saucepan along with the stock and remaining bean ingredients. Cook over a medium heat for 90 minutes, stirring occasionally. If needed, top up with extra hot stock or water during cooking.

Meanwhile, to make the mash, add the potatoes to another saucepan and cover with water. Bring to the boil and cook for around 13 minutes, or until tender when pierced with a fork.

While the potatoes are cooking, infuse the milk by adding it to a small saucepan along with the onion, garlic, bay leaf, salt and white pepper. Bring to a simmer, then take off the heat and let the flavours infuse.

When the potatoes are cooked, drain them in a colander and let them steam-dry for 2–3 minutes before transferring them to a food processor. Strain the infused milk into the processor along with the hummus, olive oil and steamed spinach. Blend for about 20 seconds. Be careful not to over-blend, as this can turn the potatoes gluey; you want a creamy, green purée. Taste and adjust the seasoning if necessary.

Once the beans are tender and cooked, purée about 1 cup of them in a blender until smooth, then stir the purée back into the pan of remaining beans and cook for another 5 minutes, to thicken.

Serve the creamy spinach and hummus mash with the rich black beans and any sides of your choice.

Le Gallois Potato Fondant

I have a love-hate relationship with this famous potato dish. I was a young 17-year-old chef thrown in at the deep end in a restaurant called Le Gallois, and before one busy Saturday-night service, my head chef asked me to whip up some fondants to go with one of the dishes on the menu. I got them prepared and into the oven 30 minutes before the first lot of diners were due to arrive. I was surprisingly well prepared before this service, after ticking off my 100 prep jobs in the afternoon. In came the first check and the head chef shouted in my direction, 'Four fondants please chef!'. By now, time had flown by and I looked at my watch – the fondants had been in the oven for well over an hour. Way longer than they should have been – my timer hadn't gone off! I shouted, 'Yes, chef!' and prayed I wouldn't be bringing out burnt blocks of potato; my heart was beating through my chest. I pulled out the fondants, peeled back the foil... and the fondants were burnt to a crisp. I wanted the whole world to swallow me up; I felt like my world was over. That's the pressure of fine-dining cooking for you. It's a lesson I won't ever forget: check the timer!

SERVES 6

4 large Vivaldi potatoes
(or any waxy baking potato)

3 tbsp extra virgin olive oil

115g (½ cup/4oz) butter

3 sprigs of thyme

2 bay leaves

1 tbsp miso paste

500ml (2 cups) vegetable stock

1 tsp sea salt

Pinch of ground white pepper

Preheat your oven to 220°C/200°C fan (425°F/Gas Mark 7).

Start by peeling the potatoes and cutting them into discs 2.5cm (1 inch) thick. Then use a small paring knife to gently round off the sharp edges of each disc (blunting the corners will ensure the fondants cook evenly).

Place a large cast-iron pan over a medium heat and add the oil. Once hot, place the potato discs in the pan, allowing them to sear on one side until golden brown. Flip and cook the other side until golden, then add the butter, thyme and bay and let the butter melt around the potatoes.

Whisk the miso paste into the stock, then pour the stock into the pan, ensuring the potatoes are partially submerged. Season with the salt and white pepper, then bring the stock to a simmer.

Cut a circular sheet of baking parchment the same size as the pan and place it directly on top of the potatoes. Cover the pan with foil, then transfer to the oven and cook for 40 minutes, until the potatoes are cooked through and the liquid has reduced.

Potato & Green Bean Salad

If you can get hold of Anya potatoes for this salad, it'll make all the difference – they're super waxy, making them hold up really well to the rest of the ingredients. If not, any other waxy potatoes will be fine. Using the brine from a ferment works a treat in the salad dressing, but if you don't have a ferment on the go, use lemon juice or vinegar.

SERVES 4

600g (21oz) Anya or other waxy new potatoes

200g (7oz) French beans, trimmed

12 pitted black olives, halved

Big handful of salad leaves (I often use rocket/arugula)

2 tbsp chopped chives

2 tbsp dill fronds or fennel tops

For the dressing

4 tbsp maple syrup

3 tbsp wholegrain mustard

4 tbsp extra virgin olive oil

4 tbsp sauerkraut brine, lemon juice or vinegar

1 tsp sea salt

Start by steaming or boiling the potatoes until tender, then allow them to cool.

To cook the beans, bring a pan of water to the boil and prepare a bowl of ice-cold water. Add the beans to the boiling water and blanch for 2 minutes, then drain and place them straight in the ice-cold water to stop them cooking. Drain again.

Add all the dressing ingredients to a small bowl and whisk to combine.

Cut the potatoes and beans into bite-sized pieces and place them in a bowl along with the remaining salad ingredients. Add the dressing, then toss everything together gently until well mixed.

Leek & Potato Soup with Macadamia & Chive Dressing

We love leeks in Wales, and we also love leek and potato soup. A leek is actually the national symbol of Wales, probably because leeks need lots of water to grow and Wales has TOO much rain! You can't beat this soup; the potatoes thicken it to a delicate, creamy consistency. It's great on its own, but paired with the nutty chive dressing and potato doughnuts for dipping (see overleaf), this will blow your mind.

SERVES 6

For the soup

4 tbsp olive oil

5 leeks, white and pale green parts roughly chopped, green tops reserved

4 garlic cloves, roughly chopped

2 celery sticks, roughly chopped

2 tsp celery salt

½ tsp ground white pepper

2 large potatoes (I recommend Maris Piper), peeled and chopped into small chunks

1 litre (4 cups) vegetable stock

250ml (1 cup) macadamia nut milk, or milk of your choice

Juice of ½ lemon, to taste

For the macadamia and chive dressing

125g (1 cup/4½oz) macadamia nuts, toasted

40g (1 cup/1½oz) chopped chives

Juice of ½ lemon

1 tbsp capers

4 tbsp extra virgin olive oil

Heat the olive oil in a large pan over a medium heat, then add the chopped leeks, garlic and celery, seasoning with the celery salt and white pepper. Stir to coat everything in the oil, then lower the heat, cover with a lid and let the vegetables sweat gently, stirring occasionally to prevent sticking. The lid will help trap moisture as the leeks soften, meaning you won't have to add as much liquid later on.

Once the vegetables are soft, add the potatoes. Stir well, then deglaze the pan with the stock. Bring to a gentle simmer, then reduce the heat and let it cook until the potatoes are soft.

While the soup is simmering, finely shred the green leek tops and, when the potatoes are ready, stir in the macadamia nut milk and the shredded greens. Let the greens cook for about 5 minutes before blitzing the soup until super smooth. Add the soup back to the pan and season with the lemon juice, and extra salt if it needs it.

For the dressing, add all the ingredients to a small food processor and blitz until roughly chopped and a little saucy.

Serve the soup topped with lashings of the dressing. My favourite way to serve these is with my potato doughnuts (see overleaf), but toasted sourdough is also lovely.

Potato & Mustard Doughnuts

These fluffy savoury doughnuts taste like so much more than the sum of their parts. I always whip up a batch if I'm making leek and potato soup (see page 58), as they are perfect for tearing and dunking, but feel free to enjoy them by themselves or serve them up with a dip like my Scotch bonnet chilli jam (page 172).

MAKES ABOUT 10

1 large (200g/7oz) Maris Piper potato, peeled and cubed

140g (1 cup/5oz) plain (all-purpose) flour

½ tsp baking powder

½ tsp bicarbonate of soda (baking soda)

4 tbsp nutritional yeast

1 tbsp Dijon mustard

1 tsp onion granules

About 60ml (¼ cup) milk

1 litre (4 cups) neutral oil, for frying

Sea salt

To make these doughnuts, you'll first need to make a mash. Add the potato to a saucepan and cover with water. Bring to the boil and cook for around 13 minutes, or until tender when pierced with a fork. When the potato is cooked, drain in a colander and let it steam-dry for 2–3 minutes, before transferring it back to the pan and mashing until smooth.

Add the mash to a bowl along with the flour, baking powder, bicarbonate of soda, nutritional yeast, mustard and onion granules. Mix well to form a dough, then add enough milk to bring it all together; you're looking for a soft, slightly sticky dough.

Heat the oil in a heavy-based skillet or large saucepan (ensuring the oil comes no further than halfway up the sides of the pan) set over a medium heat. Bring it to about 180°C (356°F). To test if the oil is hot enough, place a wooden spoon in the pan; if bubbles form around the spoon, it is hot enough to fry.

Divide the dough into about 10 equal pieces and roll each piece between your hands to form golf-ball-sized balls. In batches, carefully lower them into the hot oil and fry until golden brown and crisp on the outside. Remove from the oil with a slotted spoon or spider and drain on a plate lined with kitchen paper to remove excess oil. Season with flaky sea salt before serving.

Smashed New Potatoes

I've previously mentioned how important I think it is to have somewhere in your vegetable patch where you can spontaneously cook. This recipe is a result of that. After the delight I felt having harvested the first potatoes of the year, I decided to quickly light my outdoor oven so I could enjoy them there and then – simple, crisp and smoky, this is all about showcasing how incredible those early new potatoes can be.

SERVES 4

500g (1lb 2oz) new potatoes

4 tbsp olive oil, plus extra for drizzling

2 tsp sea salt, plus extra to serve

1 tsp cracked black pepper

1 tbsp fresh thyme leaves

1 tbsp fresh rosemary

2 tbsp fresh lavender leaves (optional)

Preheat your oven to 220°C/200°C fan (425°F/Gas Mark 7) or light your outdoor oven or pizza oven.

Place the potatoes in a baking tin or cast-iron pan, drizzle over the olive oil and sprinkle with the salt and pepper. Mix really well, then roast for 20 minutes, or until tender.

Using a potato masher or the base of a jam jar, gently squash each potato to slightly flatten them. Scatter over all the herbs and generously drizzle with more olive oil.

Roast the potatoes for a further 15 minutes until they are golden and crisp at the edges.

Sprinkle with a little extra salt, then serve hot as a side or snack with your favourite dip.

Triple-cooked Chip Butty & Pea Purée

OK, to anyone outside of the UK I'm sure this is a little obscure, but there's no denying that a chip butty (fries sandwich) is an unbelievable naughty delicacy. Soft white bread, crispy, fresh chunky chips and SAUCE! It's all about the sauce for me – I use my tomato and mushroom ketchup on page 118. Cooking the potatoes three times results in a chip that is heaven-sent – trust me on this. Dried peas make a rich pea purée like no other; when I worked in a really fancy restaurant as a young chef, despite it being spring, my head chef would insist on us still using dried marrowfat peas for our pea purée. It has a nostalgic flavour, reminiscent of trips to the chip shop as a kid. Choose good-quality rolls to stuff your chips (fries) into; however, if you want just the chips as a side, skip the butty part.

SERVES 6

4 Maris Piper potatoes (unpeeled)

2 tsp sea salt

4 tbsp olive oil

1 litre (4 cups) neutral oil, for frying

For the pea purée

170g (1 cup/6oz) dried marrowfat peas, soaked overnight

1 tsp sea salt

1 tsp liquid smoke (optional)

1 tsp miso paste

2 tsp dried mint

Juice of 1 lemon juice

To serve

6 bread rolls, split in half

Butter, for spreading

Tomato ketchup (see page 118 for homemade)

Pea shoots (optional)

Cut the potatoes into thick, even-sized chips (fries), then steam until just tender; be really careful not to overcook them. Spread the chips out on a baking tray lined with baking parchment and let them cool slightly before placing them in the fridge for 1 hour. The dry environment of the fridge will help dehydrate the surface of the chips, making them crisper when cooked.

Meanwhile, preheat your oven to 200°C/180°C fan (400°F/Gas Mark 6).

After chilling, toss the chips with the salt and olive oil, then roast in the oven for 25 minutes, or until they turn golden brown and begin to crisp up. Remove from the oven and allow to cool completely.

Meanwhile, make the pea purée. Drain the soaked peas and simmer in fresh water until soft; this should take around 45 minutes. Drain, reserving a little of the cooking water, and transfer to a blender. Add the remaining ingredients and blitz until smooth (though I like a few chunks in there, for texture), adding a little of the reserved cooking water if needed. Set aside.

Heat the oil in a heavy-based skillet or large saucepan (ensuring the oil comes no further than halfway up the sides of the pan) set over a medium heat. Bring it to about 180°C (356°F). To test if the oil is hot enough, place a wooden spoon in the pan; if bubbles form around the spoon, it is hot enough to fry. Fry the chips in batches for around 4–5 minutes, allowing them to get super golden and crisp. When cooked, remove them to a plate lined with kitchen paper to absorb excess oil.

Butter your bread rolls then dollop on some ketchup. Pile your hot chips into each bun, then top with the pea purée, and some pea shoots if you have them.

carrot

Carrot & Clementine Set Custard

These are the perfect pudding if you want to impress friends or family. With the carrot, clementine and saffron, they feel and look like a celebration of sunshine.

MAKES 4-5

125ml (½ cup) carrot juice

125ml (½ cup) orange juice

1 tsp saffron strands

1 cinnamon stick

125ml (½ cup) maple syrup

560ml (2¼ cups) coconut milk

¾ tsp agar agar powder or 1 tbsp agar agar flakes

2 clementines, peeled and segmented, or canned clementine/mandarin segments

Carrot top tips, to serve (optional)

Add the carrot juice, orange juice, saffron, cinnamon and maple syrup to a small saucepan. Place over a medium heat and bring the mixture to a gentle simmer, allowing the saffron to infuse and the juice to reduce by about a quarter. This should take about 10 minutes.

Meanwhile, heat most of the coconut milk in a separate saucepan over a medium heat, reserving a small amount in a small bowl. Whisk the agar agar into the reserved coconut milk until it is fully dissolved.

Once the coconut milk in the pan is piping hot but not boiling, pour in about three-quarters of the orange syrup, straining out the cinnamon stick, then stir well. This should transform the colour into a golden orange.

Add the agar agar mixture to the custard and, stirring continuously, allow the mixture to simmer for a few minutes, which will activate the agar agar and help the custard set. Once the mixture is well combined and slightly thickened, remove the pan from the heat. Pour into 4–5 individual panna cotta moulds and cover each one directly on the surface with cling film (plastic wrap) to stop a skin from forming. Place in the fridge for at least 3 hours to set.

While the custards are setting, gently toss the clementine segments in the remaining syrup.

When the custards are set, remove them from the moulds by running a knife around the edges and inverting and gently shaking them onto plates. If they need a little encouragement, you can dip the moulds into a bowl of hot water for a few seconds to help loosen the custard.

Serve with the clementine segments, a drizzle of the syrup and some carrot top tips, if you like.

Note
The custard shouldn't be firm like a jelly (jello) – if it is, next time reduce the amount of agar agar slightly.

Carrot Ribbon & Chard Kimchi

I am always trying to come up with ways I can use up my chard harvests; just one plant produces so much food, it's ridiculous. Its sweet and earthy flavour goes so well with carrots in this kimchi. It's quite delicate but super delicious, so it works as a side to so many dishes.

FILLS A 2-LITRE (3½-PINT) JAR

6 carrots, peeled and pared into ribbons using a swivel peeler

8 chard leaves with stalks, finely shredded

1 leek, finely chopped

10 garlic cloves, finely chopped

Thumb-sized piece of fresh ginger, peeled and finely chopped

1 sheet of dried nori seaweed, torn into small pieces (optional), plus 1 sheet for capping off the kimchi

3 tbsp light soy sauce

2 tbsp gochugaru (Korean red chilli flakes)

Sea salt

Place a large bowl on your weighing scales and set the scale to zero, then add all the ingredients except the gochugaru, salt and extra sheet of nori seaweed. Work out what 2% of the weight is, then add that weight in sea salt and the 2 tablespoons of gochugaru. Massage the ingredients together for 5 minutes or so, then cover the bowl over with a clean tea (dish) towel. Set aside for at least 2 hours so the natural brine is drawn out.

Transfer the mixture, with the brine, to a sterilized jar, leaving 2.5cm (1 inch) of headroom at the top of the jar. Make sure you've added enough brine to cover the mixture by around 1cm (½ inch). Use the sheet of nori to cap off the jar. Place a glass fermentation weight on top to hold everything beneath the brine (see page 15 for my fermentation troubleshooting guide).

Cover loosely with the jar lid or a clean tea (dish) towel and leave the kimchi to ferment out of the fridge for about 10 days. Length of fermentation will depend on the temperature of your kitchen. Optimal temperature is around 21°C (70°F). Give the brine a little taste after around the 7-day mark: when it has an acidic tang you like, place it in the fridge, where it can be stored for up to 3 months.

Check the kimchi occasionally to release gas and to look for any signs of yeast on the surface. If you see any, skim it off immediately. The kimchi underneath should still be fine.

Carrot-top Salsa Verde

Carrot tops are often overlooked...which is a big shame! They always get used up in my kitchen due to their herbaceous earthy flavour and because they are packed with vitamins C and K and minerals like calcium and potassium. Stir this dressing through pasta or use it to add life to soups and salads.

FILLS 1 SMALL JAR

Handful of carrot tops

Handful of parsley leaves

Handful of chives

3 garlic cloves

3 tbsp capers

3 cocktail gherkins

1 tbsp Dijon mustard

3 tbsp extra virgin olive oil, plus extra if needed

3 tbsp red wine vinegar

Pinch each of sea salt and cracked black pepper

Place the carrot tops, parsley, chives, garlic, capers and gherkins on your chopping board and chop really finely. A few chunky bits won't hurt, but to make it saucy you'll want it fine.

Scrape the chopped ingredients into a bowl and stir in the mustard, olive oil, vinegar, salt and pepper.

Serve right away or transfer it to a jar and cover with extra olive oil. It should keep for up to 2 weeks in the fridge if everything is fully submerged in the oil.

Carrot, Coconut & Wild Rice Salad

This is one of my dad's recipes. It's very simple but has all the flavour and texture notes that you'd want in a salad. Leftover rice can be used for ease and go heavy on the coriander!

SERVES 2-4 AS LUNCH OR A SIDE

4 tbsp extra virgin olive oil

Zest and juice of 1 lime

1 garlic clove, minced

1 tsp cumin seeds, toasted

170g (1 cup/6oz) cooked wild rice

4 carrots, peeled and grated

5 spring onions (scallions), finely sliced

Handful of coriander (cilantro) leaves, finely chopped

1 green chilli, finely sliced

4 tbsp desiccated (dried shredded) coconut

4 tbsp dried cranberries, finely chopped

In a small bowl or jug (pitcher), whisk together the olive oil, lime juice, garlic and cumin seeds to create a dressing.

Add all the remaining ingredients to a bowl and stir really well. Add the dressing and stir well again, then set the salad aside for around 10 minutes for all the flavours to get to know each other.

Serve on its own, or as a side as part of a bigger spread.

Cream of Carrot & Hazelnut Tagliatelle

When root veg like carrots are roasted in a hot oven, they of course caramelize, but their texture also completely changes from a fibrous watery root to something creamy and tender. After roasting, my carrots are blitzed with a heap of other delicious ingredients to create a creamy, luxurious sauce perfect for pasta to soak up.

SERVES 4

5 carrots

1 whole garlic bulb, halved across the circumference

1 onion, peeled and halved

5 sprigs of thyme

½ tsp smoked paprika

2 tbsp olive oil

130g (1 cup/4½oz) hazelnuts, or use cashew or macadamia nuts (or seeds for nut-free)

240ml (1 cup) hot vegetable stock

500g (1lb 2oz) dried tagliatelle

1 tsp miso paste

2 tsp Dijon mustard

5 tbsp nutritional yeast

125ml (½ cup) cashew nut milk

Sea salt and cracked black pepper

Preheat your oven to 200°C/180°C fan (400°F/Gas Mark 6).

Place the carrots in a roasting tray with the halved garlic bulb, onion, thyme, smoked paprika, olive oil and 1 teaspoon each of salt and cracked black pepper. Mix together really well, then roast in the oven for about 35 minutes, or until the carrots are soft.

Meanwhile, soak the nuts in the hot vegetable stock.

Ten minutes before the carrots are cooked, cook your pasta according to the packet instructions, until al dente.

Add the cooked carrots and onion to a blender or food processor and squeeze in the flesh from the roasted garlic bulb. Now add the soaked nuts and their stock, the miso paste, mustard, nutritional yeast and milk. Blitz until super smooth.

Drain the cooked pasta, reserving a little pasta cooking water in the pan, then stir the creamy carrot sauce through the pasta, adding seasoning if needed.

Immune-boosting Carrot Ferment

We should all know the power that eating fermented foods has on our gut. They're good for all-round health and wellness, but this ferment in particular is supercharged. In this recipe I've added age-old immune-boosting ingredients such as garlic, turmeric, cinnamon, cloves, cayenne and cardamom to create a divine sauerkraut-style ferment that'll boost your immune system through the winter months.

FILLS A 3-LITRE (5-PINT) JAR

At least 5 carrots, grated

1 small white cabbage, shredded

1 onion, finely sliced

3 tbsp minced fresh ginger

1 red chilli, finely chopped

5 garlic cloves, minced

2 bay leaves

1 tsp ground turmeric or 1 piece of fresh turmeric, finely sliced

1 cinnamon stick

1 tsp cracked black pepper

1 tsp cayenne pepper

3 cloves

2 cardamom pods

Sea salt

Add the carrots and cabbage to a bowl with the onion, ginger and chilli, then stir in the garlic, bay, turmeric, cinnamon, black pepper, cayenne, cloves and cardamom.

Weigh the contents of the bowl, work out what 2% of that weight is, then add that weight in sea salt. Massage the salt into everything for at least 5 minutes, then cover the bowl with a clean tea (dish) towel and set it aside for 2 hours for the liquid to be drawn out.

Transfer the mixture, with the brine, to a sterilized jar, leaving 2.5cm (1 inch) of headroom at the top of the jar. Make sure you've added enough brine to cover the mixture by around 1cm (½ inch). Use a slice of onion or a cabbage leaf to cap off the jar. Place a glass fermentation weight on top to hold everything beneath the brine (see page 15 for my fermentation troubleshooting guide).

Seal the jar and leave out of the fridge to ferment for up to 14 days. The speed of fermentation depends on the temperature in your kitchen; the warmer it is, the faster it is. Every now and then during fermentation, open the jar to release any gas that may have built up (unless using an airlock where the gas is naturally released).

You can assess the level of fermentation by tasting the brine. The tangier it is, the more fermented it is. Once you've reached your desired level of tang, place the ferment in the fridge. This will slow the fermentation right down and preserve it for months.

Check the ferment occasionally to release gas and to look for any signs of yeast on the surface. If you see any, skim it off immediately. The veggies underneath should still be fine.

Baby Carrot Tempura with Carrot Kimchi Emulsion

SERVES 4

For the carrot kimchi emulsion

70g (½ cup/2½oz) carrot ribbon and chard kimchi (see page 71)

125ml (½ cup) soy milk

4 tbsp rice wine vinegar or sauerkraut brine

400ml (1¾ cups) extra virgin olive or cold-pressed rapeseed (canola) oil, plus more if needed

½ tsp sea salt

For the tempura

70g (½ cup/2½oz) plain (all-purpose) flour

60g (½ cup/2¼oz) cornflour (cornstarch)

½ tsp baking powder

4 tbsp mixed black and white sesame seeds

About 375ml (1½ cups) ice-cold water

1 litre (4 cups) vegetable oil or avocado oil, for frying

10–12 baby carrots, scrubbed clean (I leave a bit of stalk on each one)

To garnish (optional)

Carrot-top salsa verde (see page 72)

Carrot seeds can be difficult to germinate, so you sow more seeds than you need to give yourself the best chance. Then, when they sprout up, you must thin them out to ensure each carrot has space to grow. I'm very bad at this because I hate to kill the little seedlings I've raised, which means when I eventually go to harvest my carrots, I'll often pull out tiddlers!

However, this dish is perfect when you have little or baby carrots. I make a clever emulsion with my carrot ribbon and chard kimchi (page 71) but you can also serve this with carrot-top salsa verde (page 72).

First up, prepare the carrot kimchi emulsion. In a tall measuring jug (pitcher), combine the kimchi, soy milk and vinegar or brine. Using a stick blender, blitz the mixture until the kimchi is roughly chopped, then continue to blitz while slowly drizzling in the oil until the mixture emulsifies into a thick, creamy mayonnaise-like consistency. If it's not as thick as you'd like, simply add a little more oil and blitz again. Taste and season with salt, then set aside until ready to serve.

To make the tempura, add the flours, baking powder and sesame seeds to a bowl and mix well. Whisk in enough ice-cold water for it to resemble a loose pancake batter consistency.

Heat the oil in a heavy-based skillet or large saucepan (ensuring the oil comes no further than halfway up the sides of the pan) set over a medium heat. Bring it to about 180°C (356°F). To test if the oil is hot enough, place a wooden spoon in the pan; if bubbles form around the spoon, it is hot enough to fry.

Dunk the carrots into the batter and then carefully transfer them into the hot oil. Fry in batches until crisp and a little golden, around 4 minutes. When ready, remove them from the pan using a spider or slotted spoon, then place on a plate lined with kitchen paper to absorb any excess oil. Season with salt, then serve them with the carrot kimchi emulsion, and a little carrot-top salsa verde as an optional extra garnish.

Smoked Carrot Kebab with Burnt Onion Purée

This dish encompasses the book for me. Taking the humble carrot and transforming it to be the star of the plate. It is a total celebration of carrot. The three cooking stages and the sweet, tangy, smoky flavours will seriously impress.

SERVES 4

10 large, thick carrots

2 large onions, quartered (unpeeled)

3 tbsp olive oil, plus extra for frying

Pinch of sea salt

125ml (1 cup) soy milk

1 tsp miso paste

Juice of ½ lemon

4 tbsp black tea leaves, for smoking (optional)

For the glaze

125ml (½ cup) maple syrup

1 tsp miso paste

4 tbsp olive oil

1 tsp sumac

½ tsp harissa spice blend

To serve

Crushed pistachios

Carrot tops

Carrot, coconut and wild rice salad (see page 75), optional

Preheat your oven to 250°C/220°C fan (475°F/Gas Mark 9), or as hot as your oven will go.

Place the whole carrots and the quartered onions in a baking dish or cast-iron pan, drizzle over the olive oil and sprinkle over the salt. Roast in the oven until the carrots are tender and the onions have slightly blackened or charred, around 20 minutes. Don't overdo the carrots as you want them tender with a bit of a bite to them, not mushy. Use a fork to check if they're done after about 15 minutes – if the onions need longer to blacken, just remove the carrots first. Once cooked, allow to cool to room temperature.

While the carrots are cooling, prepare the glaze by combining the ingredients in a bowl and whisking until smooth.

Add the blackened onions to a blender, discarding the skins, then add the milk, miso and lemon juice. Blitz to create a super-smooth purée. You may need to pass it through a fine sieve (strainer) if your blender isn't hugely powerful.

Once the carrots have cooled enough to handle, slice them lengthways very finely on a mandoline. This is a little fiddly so just take your time and be careful. Thread carrot slices onto skewers, concertinaing them as you do so. Pack and compress them onto the skewers as best as you can without breaking them.

Heat a cast-iron pan over a medium heat and, when hot, add a splash of olive oil. Place the skewers in the pan and sauté on all sides, brushing with the glaze, until caramelized (I use a rosemary sprig for this to add a little herby aroma).

Continued...

Optional next step:

You can also add an extra cooking step to the carrots – smoking them! To set up your makeshift smoking station, fill a wok with the tea leaves and place a bamboo steaming basket above it. Place the wok over a medium to low heat for the tea to start smoking. Once the carrot skewers have finished frying in the pan, transfer them to the steaming basket. Cover the steaming basket and let the skewers absorb the aromatic smoke for a few minutes, then continue with the recipe as follows.

To serve, spread a generous amount of the burnt onion purée on the plate, then add a couple of skewers. Scatter with pistachios and some carrot tops, then serve alongside the carrot, coconut and wild rice salad (or salad of your choice).

Whole Roast Carrot, Olive & Sun-dried Tomato Cream Tart

I usually make this quiche-like tart with the first carrot harvest of the year. It's a delicate, summery treat with the punch of olives and sun-dried tomatoes. Use rainbow carrots if you have them and be sure to let the tart cool completely before slicing into it.

SERVES 8

12 medium-sized rainbow carrots, peeled (tops reserved if you like)

3 tbsp olive oil

1 tsp sea salt, plus a pinch

1 x 300g (10½oz) block of silken tofu, drained

3 tbsp chickpea (gram) flour

180ml (¾ cup) soy milk

5 tbsp nutritional yeast

¼ tsp garlic granules

1 tbsp miso paste

¼ tsp ground turmeric

1 tbsp tahini

1 tsp ground black pepper

2 big handfuls of nettle or spinach leaves

Big handful of basil leaves

10 sun-dried tomatoes, finely chopped

12 pitted Kalamata olives, halved

For the pastry (or use shop-bought shortcrust pastry/pie crust)

425g (3 cups/15oz) plain (all-purpose) flour, plus extra for dusting

Pinch of sea salt

225g (1 cup/8oz) cold butter, cubed, plus extra for greasing

2 tbsp ice-cold water, plus more if needed

First up, the pastry. Place the flour, salt and butter in a large bowl. Rub the butter into the flour with your fingers until the mixture resembles breadcrumbs. Pour in the water and mix to form a ball of dough, then tip it onto your work surface and briefly knead it to bring it together. Transfer to a lidded container and chill in the fridge for 20 minutes or so.

Meanwhile, to prepare the carrots, preheat your oven to 200°C/180°C fan (400°F/Gas Mark 6). Place the carrots in a roasting tray, mix through the olive oil and pinch of salt and roast for 20 minutes. Once tender, set aside to cool.

Add the tofu to a blender with the chickpea flour, milk, nutritional yeast, garlic, miso, turmeric, tahini, and teaspoon each of salt and pepper, and blitz until smooth and creamy. Set aside.

Steam or blanch the nettle or spinach leaves, then chop super finely with the basil and reserved carrot tops (if you have them). Add this to the tofu mixture, along with the sun-dried tomatoes and olives and mix well. Set aside for later.

Grease a loose-bottomed tart tin (pan) or pie dish, about 20cm (8 inches) in diameter and 5cm (2 inches) deep.

Roll out your pastry on a sheet of lightly floured baking parchment to around 5mm (¼ inch) thick and big enough to line the tin's base and sides. Carefully lift up the parchment and pastry, then invert it into the tart tin. Gently push it into the tin to line the base and sides, then peel away the parchment and trim off any overhanging pastry.

Return the large piece of baking parchment to the centre of the pastry, then generously fill it with baking beans or uncooked rice. Place the tart tin on a baking tray and bake for 10 minutes (alongside the carrots if they are still in the oven).

Continued...

Remove the parchment and baking beans, then return the pastry case to the oven for a further 5 minutes or until the pastry is lightly golden. Leave to cool slightly.

Reduce the oven temperature to 180°C/160°C fan (350°F/Gas Mark 4).

Pour a third of the creamy tofu filling into the pastry case and smooth it out, then add a layer of roasted carrots (about 4 – halved lengthways if thick). Repeat this twice more, ending on a layer of carrots.

Bake the tart on the bottom shelf of the oven for 40–45 minutes, until golden. Allow it to cool for at least an hour on a wire rack before serving at room temperature, with a few pickles and green salad on the side.

courgette

Beer-battered Courgette Flowers Stuffed with Creamy Mushrooms

I've always said that this dish would be the first on my menu when I open up my restaurant. It's delicate and sophisticated while still being humble. Squash flowers are eaten all around the world – from Italy to South America. I stuff them with whatever mushrooms I can get my hands on at the time; shiitake work well – just make sure you really caramelize them in the pan. Feel free to swap the beer out for sparkling water if you prefer.

SERVES 4

2 tbsp olive oil

1 small onion, finely chopped

3 garlic cloves, minced

300g (3 cups/10½oz) mushrooms, finely chopped

1 x 300g (10½oz) block of silken tofu, drained

4 tbsp nutritional yeast

4 tbsp mixed soft herbs, such as basil, chives, parsley and nasturtium, finely chopped

3 tbsp tahini

3 tbsp plain (all-purpose) flour

Sea salt and cracked black pepper

For the flowers and batter

12 courgette (zucchini) or squash flowers

140g (1 cup/5oz) plain (all-purpose) flour, plus extra for dusting

250ml (1 cup) beer (lager or ale)

1 tsp baking powder

Pinch of sea salt

Vegetable oil, for frying

First place the courgette or squash flowers in a bowl of cold water; this will soften them, making them easy to open and fill.

To prepare the filling, heat the olive oil in a large pan over a medium heat. Add the onion and sauté until it becomes a little caramelized, stirring every now and then to stop it from burning. Add the garlic and continue to cook for a couple of minutes. Next, add the mushrooms to the pan and cook until they release their moisture and begin to brown, seasoning with salt and pepper.

While the mushrooms are cooking, place the silken tofu in a large bowl with the nutritional yeast, chopped herbs and tahini.

When the mushrooms are golden and slightly crispy, add them to the tofu mixture. Using a fork or whisk, beat the mixture until it is creamy and there are no tofu lumps. Finally, stir in the flour, which will help bind the filling together and firm it up when it cooks. Transfer the filling to a piping (pastry) bag and place in the fridge to chill for about 15 minutes.

Remove the courgette flowers from the water and allow them to drip dry on kitchen paper while the filling chills.

Carefully open each courgette flower and trim the stigma inside. Pipe a small amount of the filling into the centre, taking care not to overfill as you want to be able to gently fold the petals over the filling to secure it inside. Be sure to cover all the filling with the petals; no filling should be exposed. Repeat until you have filled all the flowers, then set them on a plate and leave to one side.

Now make a start on the tomato sauce by simply adding all the ingredients to a small saucepan. Bring to a simmer, then leave to simmer over a low heat while you cook the stuffed courgette flowers.

Continued...

For the simple tomato sauce

500ml (2 cups) passata
(strained tomatoes)

2 garlic cloves, peeled

6 basil leaves

½ tsp sea salt

Pinch of cracked black pepper

To serve

Basil leaves

Extra virgin olive oil

For the batter, in a bowl, whisk together the flour, beer, baking powder and pinch of salt until smooth.

Dust a little extra flour over the stuffed flowers – just enough to very lightly coat them so that the batter sticks nicely.

Heat the oil in a heavy-based skillet or large saucepan (ensuring the oil comes no further than halfway up the sides of the pan) set over a medium heat. Bring it to about 180°C (356°F). To test if the oil is hot enough, place a wooden spoon in the pan; if bubbles form around the spoon, it is hot enough to fry.

Dip each stuffed flower into the batter, ensuring it is fully coated, then gently lower the battered flowers into the hot oil, frying them in batches to avoid overcrowding the pan. Fry until golden and crispy, turning them after a couple of minutes to ensure they're golden all over. When cooked, transfer them to a plate lined with kitchen paper to drain any excess oil.

To serve, remove the garlic cloves and basil from the tomato sauce and serve the crispy flowers simply on top of the sauce, garnished with a little olive oil, fresh basil and a crack of black pepper.

Burnt Courgettes with Whipped Tofu

Charring vegetables unlocks flavour levels you won't believe, and courgettes are perfect for cooking over fire as the smoky flavour penetrates through to the flesh. Serve them with my creamy whipped tofu – it's reminiscent of ricotta cheese – and toast, bread or croissants.

SERVES 4

4 courgettes (zucchini)

3 tbsp olive oil, for brushing and drizzling

2 tbsp dried oregano

Sea salt

For the whipped tofu

1 x 300g (10½oz) block of silken tofu, drained

Zest and juice of 1 lemon

1 tsp garlic granules

3 tbsp nutritional yeast

1 tbsp miso paste

To serve

6 tbsp finely chopped chives

4 croissants or slices of toasted sourdough bread

Start by preparing the courgettes. Brush them with a little oil and season with salt. Place them over hot coals on the BBQ, allowing them to cook slowly. The key is to let them char gradually, turning them occasionally to ensure even cooking; please don't be tempted to have them over a flame, it'll just give them a non-appetizing, powdery smokiness. The heat from the coals will infuse the courgettes with a deep, smoky flavour. Take your time with this.

Meanwhile, prepare the whipped tofu. In a large bowl, combine the silken tofu with the lemon zest and juice, garlic granules, nutritional yeast, miso paste and a pinch of salt. Whisk until smooth and creamy.

Just before the courgettes are charred all over, sprinkle them with the oregano for a little aromatic note. Remove them from the heat and slice them in half lengthways.

To serve, spoon the whipped tofu onto plates and top each with a halved courgette. Generously sprinkle with the chives, then drizzle with a little more olive oil. Serve with croissants or toast on the side for scooping.

Courgette Fritters

Crispy and moreish, these fritters are perfect to cook when you're overwhelmed with courgettes from the garden! Go heavy on the mint and parsley – they add a freshness you'll really enjoy.

MAKES 8-10

2 courgettes (zucchini), grated

140g (1 cup/5oz) plain (all-purpose) flour (or use buckwheat flour for gluten free)

1 tsp baking powder

½ tsp ground cumin

½ tsp ground coriander

120ml (½ cup) sparkling water

3 spring onions (scallions), finely chopped

1 chilli, finely chopped

Handful of mint leaves, finely chopped

Handful of parsley leaves, finely chopped

Vegetable oil, for frying

Sea salt

To serve

Squeeze of lemon juice

Chopped fresh herbs

Curried courgette relish (page 107), optional

Place the grated courgettes in a colander, sprinkle with some salt and let sit for about 10 minutes. This helps to draw out excess moisture. Squeeze out as much liquid as possible from the courgettes, using a clean tea (dish) towel.

In a large bowl, combine the flour, baking powder, cumin, coriander and 1 teaspoon of salt. Mix well, then pour in the sparkling water and whisk to a thick pancake batter consistency.

Stir through the courgettes, spring onions, chilli and chopped herbs.

Heat the oil in a heavy-based skillet or large saucepan (ensuring the oil comes no further than halfway up the sides of the pan) set over a medium heat. Bring it to about 180°C (356°F). To test if the oil is hot enough, place a wooden spoon in the pan; if bubbles form around the spoon, it is hot enough to fry.

Carefully add a few large spoonfuls of the batter to the hot oil, being careful not to overcrowd the pan. Fry for a few minutes on each side, or until golden brown and crispy.

Remove the fritters to a plate lined with kitchen paper to drain any excess oil while you fry the rest of the batter.

To serve, pile the fritters onto a serving dish, squeeze over a little lemon juice and sprinkle with flaky salt. Generously scatter over some fresh herbs, then serve with my curried courgette relish or your favourite dipping sauce.

Courgette Kimchi

With this kimchi-style ferment I make a rich paste that clings on to every piece of courgette really nicely. Don't cut the courgette too fine, as you really want some bite. Feel free to add extra nori to the paste too for a 'taste of the sea' flavour!

FILLS A 3-LITRE (5-PINT) JAR

At least 4 courgettes (zucchini), cut into batons

As many courgette or squash flowers as you can get your hands on, finely sliced into ribbons

Sea salt

1 sheet of dried nori seaweed, for capping off the kimchi

Per courgette

2 spring onions (scallions), roughly chopped

1 garlic clove

1 tsp minced fresh ginger

1 tbsp light soy sauce

1 tsp sugar

1 tsp Korean red chilli flakes (gochugaru)

Place a large bowl on your weighing scales and set the scale to zero, then add the courgette batons and sliced flowers.

Add the appropriate amount of spring onions, garlic, ginger, soy sauce, sugar and chilli flakes to a food processor, based on how many courgettes you have used, and blitz until it forms a smooth paste. Stir the paste through the courgettes and flowers, then take note of the weight on the scale. Work out what 3% of the weight is, then add that weight in salt.

Massage the ingredients together for 5 minutes or so, then cover the bowl with a clean tea (dish) towel and set aside for at least 2 hours to draw out the liquid.

Transfer the mixture, with the brine, to a sterilized jar, leaving 2.5cm (1 inch) of headroom at the top of the jar. Make sure you've added enough brine to cover the mixture by around 1cm (½ inch). Use the sheet of nori to cap off the jar. Place a glass fermentation weight on top to hold everything beneath the brine (see page 15 for my fermentation troubleshooting guide).

Cover loosely with the jar lid or a clean tea towel and leave the kimchi to ferment out of the fridge for about 7–10 days. Length of fermentation will depend on the temperature of your kitchen. Optimal temperature is around 21°C (70°F). Give the brine a little taste after around the 5-day mark: when it has an acidic tang you like, seal the jar and place it in the fridge, where it can be stored for up to 3 months.

Check the kimchi occasionally to release gas and to look for any signs of yeast on the surface. If you see any, skim it off immediately. The kimchi underneath should still be fine.

Chinese-style Kimchi pancakes

If, like me, you always have a few different kimchis on the go, these pancakes are a great way to put them to delicious use. I like to serve these up on a platter for everyone to get stuck in tearing and dipping.

MAKES 6-8

425g (3 cups/15oz) plain (all-purpose) flour, plus extra for dusting

½ tsp baking powder

1 tsp sea salt

350ml (1½ cups) warm water

130g (1 cup/4½oz) courgette kimchi (page 98), finely chopped

1 tbsp sesame oil, plus extra for frying

To serve

Sliced spring onions (scallions)

Sesame seeds

Light soy sauce

Combine the flour, baking powder and salt in a large bowl.

Gradually stir in the warm water until a rough dough forms. Transfer to a lightly floured surface and knead the dough for 3–4 minutes until smooth and elastic. The dough will be on the tacky side, but don't be tempted to add too much additional flour or the pancakes will be stiff.

Transfer the dough back to the bowl, cover with a tea (dish) towel and let it rest for about 30 minutes in the fridge.

Meanwhile, finely chop the courgette kimchi until it reaches a texture similar to a coarse paste (you can also do this in a food processor). Be sure not to have any large lumps as they'll puncture the delicate dough.

After the dough has rested, divide it into 6–8 equal portions.

Lightly flour your work surface to prevent the dough from sticking, then roll 1 portion out into a long rectangle shape, as thinly as possible. Brush the dough with a little sesame oil, then apply a thin layer of chopped kimchi over the whole rectangle. Roll the dough up widthways into a long sausage, trying to roll it as tightly as possible to result in more layers.

Grab one end of the roll and coil it up into a spiral, like a snail shell. Now, using your rolling pin, roll the spiral into a flat disc, around 5mm (¼ inch) thick. Place the pancake on a piece of baking parchment and set aside while you roll and shape the remaining dough portions.

To cook the pancakes, heat a skillet or frying pan over a medium heat and add a little sesame oil. Once the oil is hot, add a pancake and cook for a few minutes on each side until golden brown and crispy. Repeat with the remaining pancakes, adding more oil to the skillet or pan as needed.

Serve the flaky pancakes hot, scattered with spring onions and sesame seeds, with soy sauce on the side for dipping.

Courgette, Lavender & Rye Oat Cookies

Another recipe that came about when I was overwhelmed with courgettes from the garden. You'll just have to trust me on this – it works great and the courgette adds a moistness to each bite. Rye offers a nutty flavour, and lavender a delicate floral note. They store for ages and are pretty healthy!

MAKES 9

130g (1 cup/4½oz) courgette (zucchini), grated

90g (1 cup/3¼oz) rolled oats

140g (1 cup/5oz) rye flour

1 tsp baking powder

½ tsp ground cinnamon

2 tbsp dried lavender flowers, plus a few extra to decorate

Pinch of sea salt

60ml (¼ cup) extra virgin olive oil

125ml (½ cup) maple syrup

Zest and juice of 1 lemon

3 tbsp crunchy nut butter of your choice (or tahini for nut free)

Preheat the oven to 200°C/180°C fan (400°F/Gas Mark 6). Line a baking sheet with baking parchment.

Squeeze out as much liquid as possible from the grated courgette, using a clean tea (dish) towel.

In a large bowl, combine the oats, flour, baking powder, cinnamon, lavender and salt.

In a separate bowl, mix the olive oil, maple syrup, lemon zest and juice and nut butter until well combined, then stir in the grated courgette. Gradually add the dry ingredients to the wet ingredients, mixing until just combined.

Dollop spoonfuls of the dough onto the lined baking sheet, spacing them about 5cm (2 inches) apart, and spread them into rounds with the back of the spoon.

Bake for 15–20 minutes, or until the edges are golden brown and the cookies are set. Let cool on the baking sheet for a few minutes before transferring to a wire rack to cool completely.

Sprinkle over a few lavender flowers to decorate and enjoy over the next few days, storing them in an airtight container.

Courgette, Leek, White Bean & Kale Stew

I'd happily (and do) live off stews like this. I call them 'gardeners' dinners' and usually don't write recipes down for them – they're just made with whatever I've harvested that day. This one is full of complementary ingredients that will nourish your heart and soul.

SERVES 4

2 leeks

4 tbsp olive oil, plus extra for drizzling

1 celery stick, finely diced

1 carrot, peeled and finely diced

5 garlic cloves, minced

1 tbsp finely chopped rosemary leaves

1 bay leaf

½ tsp smoked paprika

2 tsp sea salt

1 tsp cracked black pepper

250ml (1 cup) white wine

1 litre (4 cups) vegetable stock

510g (3 cups/1lb 2oz) cooked or canned cannellini beans

2 courgettes (zucchini), sliced into rounds (I use a yellow and a green)

Handful of parsley leaves, roughly chopped

2 big handfuls of curly or Tuscan kale

Zest of 1 lemon, to serve

Trim the leeks, then finely slice the white parts, reserving the green parts. Heat half the olive oil in a large pot over a medium heat, then add the leek whites, celery and carrot. Cook for a few minutes, then when the vegetables begin to soften, add the garlic, rosemary, bay leaf, smoked paprika, salt and pepper.

Cook for a few more minutes, then deglaze the pot with the wine, scraping the bottom of the pot with a wooden spoon to release any tasty bits. Let the wine simmer and reduce slightly, then add the stock and beans, stirring everything together. Allow the stew to come to a gentle boil, then reduce the heat to a simmer.

Let the stew bubble away for 20 minutes, then transfer half the mixture to a blender. Blitz until smooth and creamy, then return it to the pot, stirring it back into the remaining stew. This will give the stew a creamy, luxurious consistency.

Keep cooking the stew over a low heat while you prepare the courgettes. Heat the remaining olive oil in a skillet or frying pan over a high heat, add the courgettes and fry until golden brown and slightly caramelized. Meanwhile, very finely chop the reserved leek greens.

Stir the courgettes into the stew, along with the parsley, leek greens and kale.

When the kale is just cooked, serve up the stew into bowls and garnish with lemon zest and a little drizzle of olive oil.

Curried Courgette Relish

This is a go-to relish that can be used in so many ways: inside sandwiches, burgers, as a side or with cheese and crackers. It tastes a bit like piccalilli but with more of a kick!

FILLS A 2-LITRE (3½-PINT) JAR

1 large onion, finely chopped

3 tbsp olive oil

2 tsp curry powder

1 tbsp mustard seeds

1 tsp ground turmeric

1 tsp ground coriander

¼ tsp ground cloves

1 bay leaf

5 courgettes (zucchini), diced

2 green apples, peeled, cored and diced

2 red chillies, deseeded and finely chopped

250ml (1 cup) white wine vinegar

80g (½ cup/3oz) golden raisins

105g (½ cup/3¾oz) brown sugar

1 tsp sea salt

In a large, heavy-based pot or saucepan, sauté the onion in the oil until soft. Add the curry powder, mustard seeds, turmeric, coriander, ground cloves and bay leaf and cook for another minute, allowing the spices to toast slightly.

Stir through the courgettes, apples, chillies, vinegar, raisins, sugar and salt. Bring to a simmer, then allow to bubble away over a low heat for 30 minutes, stirring every now and then.

Once the relish is jammy, transfer it to a sterilized jar and seal. When cool, store in the fridge for up to 3 months. It's great as a condiment with most dishes, or in sandwiches.

Fermented Nut Stuffed Courgette Flowers

This recipe explores another side to fermentation. In case you're not aware, you can actually make something very similar to cheese using the power of fermentation and nuts! Make the 'cheese' even if you don't have flowers to stuff, and you won't regret it. It takes time but you'll be amazed at the results. Experiment with different nuts too, as each one will add a different flavour note. Make sure you use a really powerful blender to get the nut paste as smooth as possible – add additional water while blending if you feel it needs it.

SERVES 2-4

130g (1 cup/4½oz) raw cashew nuts, soaked in water for at least 2 hours

60ml (¼ cup) filtered water

5 tbsp nutritional yeast

1 tsp onion granules

1 tsp garlic granules

Juice of ½ lemon

1 tsp white miso paste

1 probiotic capsule, such as acidophilus

½ tsp celery salt

6–8 courgette (zucchini) flowers

To serve

Sourdough toast

Finely sliced red onion

Lemon zest

Extra virgin olive oil

Start by draining the soaked cashews (it's important they have soaked for at least 2 hours to soften properly). Then, in a high-speed blender, combine the drained cashews with the filtered water, nutritional yeast, onion and garlic granules, lemon juice, miso paste, probiotic capsule and celery salt. Blend until very smooth. This might take a few minutes and you will have to scrape down the sides of the blender with a spatula to help the blender out.

When super smooth, transfer the mixture to a nut milk bag or sheet of cheesecloth. In a warm, dry place where it won't be disturbed, use string and a wooden spoon to suspend the mixture in a large bowl so any liquid can slowly drip out. Cover the bowl with cling film (plastic wrap) and leave to ferment for 48 hours. The fermentation time can vary depending on the room temperature and how tangy you'd like it; the ideal temperature is 23°C (73°F). Taste the mixture – it should be tangy and very savoury.

Fill a bowl with cold water and add a few ice cubes.

Gently steam the courgette flowers in a bamboo basket for 45 seconds, then remove them from the heat and transfer to the ice-cold water to stop them cooking.

Transfer the fermented nut mixture to a piping (pastry) bag and pipe it into each flower.

Place a few stuffed flowers on freshly toasted sourdough, then scatter with red onion and lemon zest. Drizzle with a little olive oil, then tuck in.

tomato

Cream of Tomato, Fennel & Lemongrass Soup

The flavours of this soup were inspired by the fragrance of a massaman curry. A bold twist on an all-time classic soup.

SERVES 4

3kg (6lb 10oz) tomatoes (I use any that I have a glut of in summer), cut into chunks

2 fennel bulbs, cut into chunks

4 tbsp olive oil

2 leeks, finely chopped

5 garlic cloves, minced

1 tbsp minced fresh ginger

1 carrot, finely chopped

1 lemongrass stick, bashed

1 tsp ground cumin

1 tsp ground coriander

1 tsp ground cinnamon

½ tsp ground cardamom

¼ tsp ground nutmeg

3 tbsp tomato paste

1 tbsp peanut butter

1 tbsp coconut sugar, or to taste

2 sheets of dried nori seaweed, crumbled into small pieces

3 tbsp soy sauce

1 x 400g (14oz) can of coconut milk

1 star anise

About 500ml (2 cups) vegetable stock (optional)

Sea salt

Preheat your oven to 220°C/200°C fan (425°F/Gas Mark 7).

Place the tomatoes and fennel chunks in a roasting tray, drizzle over a little of the olive oil and add a sprinkling of salt. Toss them together and roast in the oven for 25–30 minutes, until caramelized.

When the tomatoes have been roasting for 5–10 minutes, heat the rest of the olive oil in a large saucepan over a medium heat. Add the leeks, garlic, ginger and carrot and sauté until softened, then add the lemongrass and spices and let them cook out for a couple of minutes, to release their fragrance. Stir in the tomato paste, peanut butter, sugar, nori and soy sauce, scraping any bits off the bottom of the pan.

Add most of the roasted tomatoes (reserving a few for garnish) and the fennel to the saucepan, along with all the juices in the tray, then pour in the coconut milk and add the star anise. Stir really well, then place a lid on the pan and let the soup simmer away for 15–20 minutes.

Remove the lemongrass and star anise, then blend the soup until smooth and creamy. Check the consistency – if you want a looser soup, add some stock and blend again. If your blender isn't super powerful, simply pass it through a fine sieve (strainer) to get a velvety consistency. Return the soup to the saucepan and check it for seasoning.

Serve garnished with the reserved roasted tomatoes, and your choice of bread.

Crumpets con Tomate

A simple but delicious dish from Catalonia, and with homegrown tomatoes there's nothing better (I use a tomato variety with lots of flesh and less pulp). You can just do this dish the traditional way with toasted bread slices, but my homemade crumpets match up a treat with the tangy tomato sauce, creating the perfect breakfast.

MAKES 8-10 CRUMPETS

450ml (scant 2 cups) warm water

1 tsp dried fast action yeast

Pinch of sea salt

4 tbsp extra virgin olive oil, plus extra for cooking

425g (3 cups/15oz) strong white bread flour

For the tomato topping

2 beef tomatoes

1 tbsp sherry vinegar, or your vinegar of choice

2 tbsp extra virgin olive oil

Pinch each of sea salt and cracked black pepper

To serve

4–5 garlic cloves, peeled

The night before cooking, whisk the water, yeast, salt and oil together in a large bowl, then fold through the flour. Stir really well for around 4 minutes, making sure the batter is super smooth. Cover the bowl and place in the fridge overnight.

The next morning, remove the bowl from the fridge and allow it to warm to room temperature, then preheat a cast-iron pan over a low–medium heat and add a little olive oil. When the pan is hot, pour in about 6 tablespoons of batter. Use a spatula to spread the batter into a neat circle, around 8cm (3 inches) in diameter (you can also use a greased metal ring or a cookie cutter placed in the pan, to make the crumpets even neater – simply fill them halfway up with the batter).

Cook for 5 minutes on each side until crisp and golden, then remove from the pan. Repeat to use up all the batter.

When the crumpets are cooked, grate the tomatoes into a small bowl and stir through the vinegar, olive oil and seasoning.

Halve and toast the crumpets, then directly rub a garlic clove on the cut surface of each crumpet. Top with lashings of the tomato mixture and serve.

Dried Tomatoes

What if I told you that you could be enjoying your summer tomatoes in the cold of winter? Well, that's what I do with my tomatoes; drying them preserves them for months. It can be done in a low-temperature oven instead of a dehydrator, but I really recommend investing in a simple countertop dehydrator.

Slice some ripe (preferably organic) tomatoes finely and place them on your dehydrator sheets. Set the temperature of your dehydrator to 40°C (104°F) and dry for 24 hours.

You can also use your oven for this; just set it to 90°C (200°F/Gas Mark ¼) and lay the tomato slices out on baking parchment, then bake until completely dry, around 4 hours.

Store in a jar and add to soups, sauces or stews, for a tangy flavour. I also eat them as a tasty sweet snack.

Charred Tomato & Mushroom Ketchup

Everyone needs a proper ketchup recipe up their sleeve, packed with rich, sweet flavours. I always use mushrooms in my ketchup to add a depth of flavour that complements the tomatoes perfectly. Splodge into sandwiches, have it with chips/fries (see page 65) and pop a bottle on the table to go alongside a cooked breakfast. I tend to remove the black gills from the mushrooms before using them, otherwise they turn the ketchup a muddy brown colour.

MAKES ABOUT 1 LITRE (2 PINTS)

3–4kg (6lb 10oz–8lb 13oz) tomatoes (juicy beef tomatoes, or any with lots of flesh)

4 portobello mushrooms, black gills removed

5 tbsp olive oil

2 onions, finely chopped

10 garlic cloves, finely chopped

500ml (2 cups) white wine vinegar

200g (1 cup/7oz) light brown sugar or coconut sugar

250ml (1 cup) maple syrup

2 bay leaves

1 tsp ground allspice

2 tsp smoked paprika

3 tsp sea salt

Preheat the BBQ or fire pit, and let the fire burn down to get some white-hot coals. Place the tomatoes directly on the grill and cook, turning occasionally, until their skins are blackened and blistered.

Remove them to a bowl and cover the bowl with a plate to lock in the steam, making the tomatoes easier to peel. Once cool enough to handle, peel off the charred skins and roughly chop the flesh.

Finely chop the mushrooms after removing the black gills. Heat a large, heavy-based pot over a medium heat and add the olive oil. Add the onions, garlic and mushrooms and sauté until the onions are soft and the mushrooms have cooked down.

Add the chopped tomatoes, followed by the vinegar, sugar and maple syrup. Add the bay leaves, allspice, smoked paprika and salt, stir well to combine and bring the mixture to a simmer. Reduce the heat to low and let it cook for at least an hour, stirring occasionally, to allow the mixture to reduce and thicken.

Once the ketchup is thick and sticky, remove the bay leaves and use a hand-held blender (or transfer the mixture to a jug blender in batches) to blitz until super smooth.

Return the blended ketchup to the pot, adjusting the seasoning if necessary. If it is too runny, you can continue to reduce it. If you need to make it smoother, simply pass it through a fine sieve (strainer).

Let cool before transferring the ketchup to sterilized bottles. It will store in the fridge for up to 3 months.

Stuffed Tomatoes

I've been known to grow some giant tomatoes at my homestead, which excites me because they're perfect for stuffing. The skin blisters and the juice transforms into a lovely dressing. My filling comprises rich flavours that together have a very meaty texture. Try to fit as much filling into each tomato as you can – if you have any left over it can be used in salads or as a side.

SERVES 4

6 large beef tomatoes

3 tbsp olive oil, plus extra
for roasting

1 small onion, finely diced

4 garlic cloves, minced

400g (14oz) mixed mushrooms,
finely chopped

6 dried apricots, finely chopped

1 preserved lemon,
finely chopped

1 tsp smoked paprika

1 tsp ground cumin

1 tbsp dried oregano

60g (½ cup/2¼oz) mixed nuts,
finely chopped

195g (1 cup/7oz) cooked
long-grain rice

Handful of basil leaves,
finely chopped

Handful of mint leaves

Sea salt and cracked black pepper

Preheat your oven to 200°C/180°C fan (400°F/Gas Mark 6).

Carefully slice off the top of each tomato and set the tops aside. Scoop out the flesh from each tomato using a teaspoon, being careful not to pierce the outer walls. Reserve the pulp, then lightly salt the insides of the tomatoes and place them upside down on a plate.

Place a large frying pan over a medium heat and add the olive oil. Add the onion and sauté until caramelized. Add the garlic and mushrooms and sauté for at least 10 minutes until golden and all the mushroom liquid has evaporated – you want the mushrooms to release all their moisture as they cook down.

Add the dried apricots, preserved lemon and reserved tomato pulp to the pan. Add the paprika, cumin and oregano, stirring well and allowing the mixture to cook for a few minutes.

Stir in the nuts, cooked rice, basil and mint, and season with salt and black pepper. Remove the pan from the heat and allow the mixture to cool slightly.

Carefully spoon the mushroom filling into the scooped-out tomatoes, packing it in gently. Place the tomato tops back on and arrange them in a baking dish.

Drizzle a little oil over the stuffed tomatoes, season with a little more salt and then bake in the oven for 20–25 minutes, until slightly blistered.

Serve up right away, with a salad of your choice.

Tomato & Nasturtium Kimchi

I am telling you, this dish is the most flavoursome recipe in the whole book. Tomatoes when fermented are supercharged; they become more tangy and umami than you could ever imagine. I'm not kidding – I am addicted to the stuff. I actually use most of the tomatoes that I grow in my garden making this tomato kimchi just to feed my habit over the cold months. I put it on pretty much everything I eat. Please try this recipe – your mind will be blown. Because of its deep flavour I actually use it to marinate and season dishes too; check out the tomato kimchi fried tofu overleaf.

FILLS A 2-LITRE (3½-PINT) JAR

1kg (2lb 3oz) tomatoes, cut into bite-sized pieces

Large handful of nasturtium leaves and flowers (or use coriander/cilantro), roughly chopped

1 large onion

Thumb-sized piece of ginger, peeled and finely chopped

6 garlic cloves, peeled

3 tbsp soy sauce

1 tbsp miso paste

4 tbsp Korean red chilli flakes (gochugaru) or other chilli (red pepper) flakes of your choice

Sea salt

Place a large bowl on your weighing scales and set to zero. Add the tomatoes and nasturtium leaves/flowers to the bowl.

Slice a side of the onion off to use a layer as the kimchi 'plug', then roughly chop the rest of the onion and add it with the ginger, garlic, soy sauce and miso paste to a food processor and blitz to a smooth paste. Stir the paste through the tomatoes, along with the chilli flakes. Weigh the mixture and calculate 2% of the weight, then add that amount of sea salt.

Stir the ingredients together really well, then cover the bowl with a clean tea (dish) towel and set aside for at least 1 hour so the natural brine is drawn out.

Transfer the mixture, with the brine, to a sterilized jar, leaving 2.5cm (1 inch) of headroom at the top of the jar. Make sure you've added enough brine to cover the mixture by around 1cm (½ inch). Use the slice of onion to cap off the jar. Place a glass fermentation weight on top to hold everything beneath the brine (see page 15 for my fermentation troubleshooting guide).

Leave to ferment out of the fridge for about 5–7 days. The length of fermentation will depend on the temperature of your kitchen – optimal temperature is around 21°C (70°F). Give the brine a little taste after around the 5-day mark; when it has an acidic tang you like, place it in the fridge, where it can be stored for up to 3 months.

Tomato Kimchi Fried Tofu

After trying this, my good friend said he could eat a whole bucket of this fried tofu: nuggets of joy! The kimchi caramelizes up really nicely around each piece of crispy tofu. I serve mine with cooling yogurt and spring onions but a little rice and veg would make it a complete meal.

SERVES 2

160g (1 cup/5½oz) tomato kimchi (see page 122)

2 tbsp sesame oil

4 tbsp maple syrup

1 x 300g (10½oz) block of extra-firm tofu, drained

6 tbsp cornflour (cornstarch)

4 tbsp neutral oil, for frying

To serve

Cooked rice

Coconut yogurt

Sliced spring onions (scallions)

Add the kimchi, sesame oil and maple syrup to a food processor and blitz to a smooth paste.

Pat the tofu dry with kitchen paper, then tear it into really rough, bite-sized chunks and place into a bowl.

Dust the tofu with the cornflour and toss together, making sure each piece is well coated.

Place a large cast-iron pan over a medium heat and add the oil for frying. When hot, add the tofu and fry until really golden and crisp – invest some time in this, turning the tofu every now and then.

Turn the heat down to low and add the kimchi paste. Stir really well, allowing the paste to caramelize around each piece of tofu. This should take around 4–5 minutes.

When the sauce has melded into each piece of tofu, serve up with rice and coconut yogurt and top with sliced spring onions.

Tomato Broth

This recipe shows just how much depth and richness tomatoes can add to dishes. I first discovered using tomatoes as a base in broths at Ivan Ramen in NYC, a famous ramen restaurant. I was so surprised at the richness and depth that their totally plant-based broth had that I had to give the technique a go for myself. The tomatoes, cooked down for some time and allowed to blister, caramelize and create a richness similar to meat. You can eat it before straining as a soup, or strain it and use it as a ramen broth.

SERVES 4

2 tbsp sesame oil

12 cherry tomatoes

1 onion, quartered

2 celery sticks, roughly chopped

1 leek, roughly chopped

2 carrots, roughly chopped

1 lemongrass stick, bashed

1 chilli, halved

4 garlic cloves, minced

Thumb-sized piece of
fresh ginger

60ml (¼ cup) Chinese rice wine

3 tbsp tomato paste

4 tbsp soy sauce

1.5 litres (6 cups) vegetable stock

1 star anise

15g (½ cup/½oz) dried shiitake mushrooms

2 sheets of dried nori seaweed,
or 7g (¼ cup/¼oz) kombu

4 tbsp miso paste

Sea salt

Place a large saucepan over a medium heat and add the sesame oil, followed by the cherry tomatoes. Cook for 5–10 minutes, letting them blister (this will create the ultimate depth to your broth). Add the onion, celery, leek and carrots.

Sauté for 15 minutes or until everything is golden brown and has melted down. Add the lemongrass, chilli, garlic, ginger and a pinch of salt. Keep sautéing for a few minutes before deglazing the pan with the rice wine, tomato paste and soy sauce.

Cook for another 2 minutes, before adding the stock, star anise, dried mushrooms and nori.

Let the broth bubble away for at least 90 minutes over a low heat, stirring every now and then, then strain through a fine sieve (strainer) into a jug (pitcher) and stir through the miso paste until it is completely dissolved.

Use straight away (see the introduction) or store in the fridge for up to 1 week.

Tomato & Butter Bean Summer Salad

This truly is my summer harvest on a plate; tomatoes straight from the greenhouse ripened by the warm sun, refreshing cucumber and a ton of homegrown herbs make the best salad for a hot day.

SERVES 4

4 large, juicy tomatoes

3 garlic cloves, peeled

1 cucumber

400g (2 cups/14oz) canned or cooked butter beans

1 red onion, finely chopped

12 pitted Kalamata olives

Large handful of mixed soft herbs, such as chives, parsley and basil, finely chopped

Zest and juice of 1 lemon

1 red chilli, finely chopped

4 tbsp nutritional yeast

5 tbsp pumpkin seeds

4 tbsp pine nuts

5 tbsp extra virgin olive oil

Cut one of the tomatoes into chunks and place in a food processor with the garlic. Blitz to a purée, then add to a bowl.

Cut the remaining tomatoes and the cucumber into bite-sized pieces and add to the bowl, along with the rest of the ingredients. Mix everything up really well and enjoy on a hot summer's day.

Tomato, Thyme & Almond Upside Down Cake

This dish is neither sweet nor savoury, but somewhere in the middle. It's a little fiddly and sometimes the results can be more on the rustic side (especially when your tomatoes are super juicy and ripe), but the flavours are always perfect. I recommend using under-ripe tomatoes that are just turning red, as they're a bit firmer and hold their shape more. Don't be tempted to turn the cake out right away – allow at least 25 minutes for the cake to cool and set slightly before turning it out.

SERVES 6

200g (1½ cups/7oz) almond flour or ground almonds

140g (1 cup/5oz) plain (all-purpose) flour (or a gluten-free flour)

2 tsp baking powder

1 tsp bicarbonate of soda (baking soda)

1 tsp fine sea salt

1 tbsp thyme leaves

250ml (1 cup) almond milk

125ml (½ cup) extra virgin olive oil, plus extra for greasing

2 tbsp white wine vinegar

5 tbsp maple syrup

4 tbsp chia seeds

Natural yogurt or crème fraîche, to serve

For the topping

350g (12½oz) cherry tomatoes, halved

4 tbsp olive oil, plus extra to serve

3 tbsp balsamic vinegar

3 tbsp maple syrup

2 tbsp thyme leaves, plus extra to garnish

Pinch of sea salt

Preheat your oven to 200°C/180°C fan (400°F/Gas Mark 6).

Grease a 23cm (9-inch) cake tin (pan) – I use a loose-bottomed tin, but this can also be cooked in a cast-iron pan.

For the topping, add all the ingredients to a bowl, toss together really well, then spread them out in the base of your prepared cake tin, making sure they cover the entire base and are in an even layer.

Clean out the bowl, then add the almond flour, plain flour, baking powder, bicarbonate of soda, salt and thyme, and mix. In a jug (pitcher), whisk together the milk, olive oil, vinegar and maple syrup, then stir in the chia seeds and let them soak for a few minutes.

Pour the wet mixture into the dry ingredients and stir until just combined, then pour the batter over the tomatoes in the tin and spread it out evenly with a rubber spatula.

Give the tin a little tap on the work surface to release any trapped air pockets, then transfer to the oven and bake until gold and firm on top, around 35 minutes, or when a skewer inserted in the middle comes out clean.

Let cool slightly in the tin before turning it out carefully onto a serving plate.

Garnish with some extra thyme leaves and olive oil and serve with yogurt or crème fraîche.

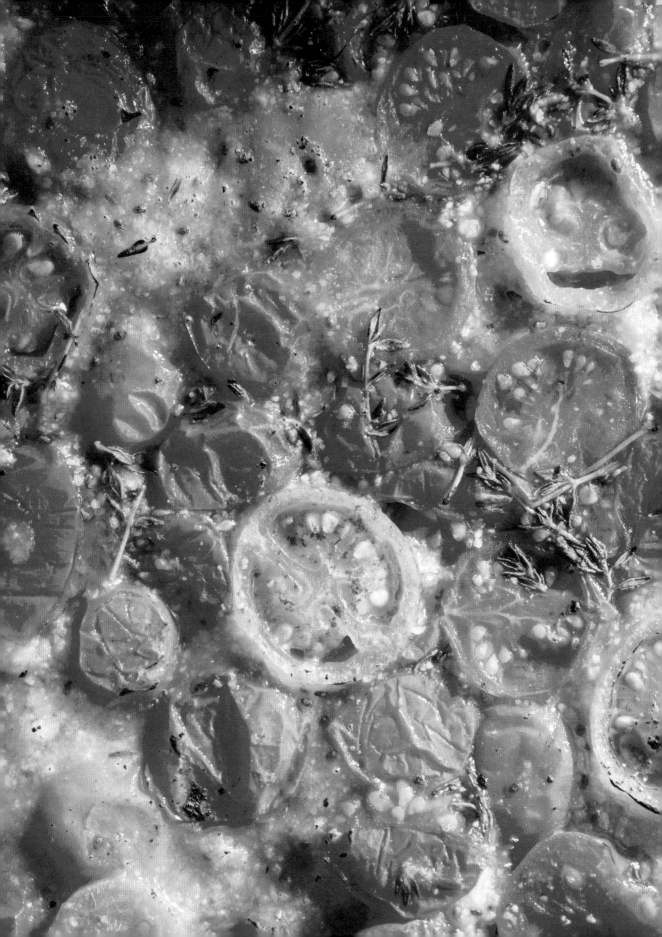

beetroot

Beetroot & Black Bean Brownie

This is actually my pre- or post-workout snack, packed full of ingredients that nourish my body. The beetroots, black beans and chocolate come together to make a super-rich brownie that also stores for up to a week, so you can grab and go!

MAKES 9

140g (5oz) cooked beetroot (beet)

170g (1 cup/6oz) canned or cooked black beans

125ml (½ cup) tahini

120ml (½ cup) olive oil

60ml (¼ cup) maple syrup

3 tsp vanilla extract

½ tsp sea salt

2 tsp ground cinnamon

2 tbsp maca powder (optional)

80g (½ cup/3oz) dark (bittersweet) chocolate chips

4 tbsp hemp seeds

4 tbsp chia seeds

100g (½ cup/3½oz) cacao powder

1 tsp baking powder

4 tbsp hazelnuts, finely chopped

4 tbsp pumpkin seeds

To decorate

Melted dark (bittersweet) chocolate

Sea salt flakes

Preheat your oven to 200°C/180°C fan (400°F/Gas Mark 6). Line a 20cm (8-inch) square baking tin (pan) with baking parchment.

Add the beetroot, black beans, tahini, olive oil, maple syrup and vanilla to your food processor and blitz until smooth. Transfer to a bowl, then fold in the remaining ingredients, except the hazelnuts and pumpkin seeds.

Pour the batter into the lined baking tin and smooth the top with a spatula. Sprinkle over the chopped hazelnuts and pumpkin seeds and bake in the oven for 25–30 minutes, until the hazelnuts are golden brown.

Remove from the oven, drizzle over some melted dark chocolate and add a sprinkle of sea salt. Allow it to cool in the tin for at least 10 minutes (this makes them easier to cut) before slicing into about 9 squares.

The brownies will store in the fridge for up to a week or in the freezer for 3 months.

Beetroot & Blackberry BBQ Sauce

I really love food alliteration that tastes good too! When blackberries come around, my mum and I usually pick a load and freeze them for the winter months. This sauce transforms them into a sticky and tangy BBQ sauce that you can use as a marinade or as a dip. The beetroots add a deep earthy flavour and colour that is very unique.

MAKES ABOUT ½ LITRE (1 PINT)

3 uncooked beetroots (beets)

3 tbsp olive oil, plus extra for sautéing

1 onion, finely chopped

4 garlic cloves, finely chopped

1 chilli (I like using a hot Scotch bonnet or similar), chopped

2 tsp mustard seeds

1 tsp fennel seeds

1 tsp cumin seeds

1 tsp ground coriander

2 tsp smoked paprika

1 tsp celery salt

3 tbsp tomato paste

1 tbsp miso paste

1 tbsp finely chopped sage leaves

1 tbsp finely chopped thyme leaves

360g (3 cups/12½oz) blackberries

60ml (¼ cup) maple syrup

125ml (½ cup) white wine vinegar

2 bay leaves

1 star anise

Sea salt

Preheat your oven to 200°C/180°C fan (400°F/Gas Mark 6).

Peel the beetroots, then cut them into very small cubes or fine dice. Place on a roasting tray, drizzle over the olive oil and a little salt and then roast in the oven for 30 minutes or so.

Meanwhile, heat a little oil in a saucepan and sauté the onion, garlic and chilli with a little salt, until golden and caramelized. Add all the spices and let them toast for a minute before stirring through the tomato and miso pastes.

Add the chopped sage and thyme, followed by the blackberries, and stir well. Cook for a few minutes before adding the roasted beetroot, maple syrup, vinegar, bay leaves and star anise. Add a pinch more salt, then pop a lid on and cook over a low heat for 30 minutes, stirring frequently, until thickened and sticky.

Transfer the sauce to sterilized jars; it will keep in the fridge for up to 6 weeks.

Beetroot & Cardamom Ice Cream

Beetroot and cardamom are a classic combination of fragrant and earthy flavours, and paired here they create a vibrant ice cream.

MAKES JUST OVER 1 LITRE (2 PINTS)

For the syrup

1 uncooked beetroot (beet), peeled and grated

250ml (1 cup) maple syrup

For the ice cream base

2 x 400g (14oz) cans of coconut milk

3 cardamom pods, crushed

1 vanilla pod, split lengthways, or 2 tbsp vanilla bean paste

250ml (1 cup) cashew nut milk, or milk of your choice

5 tbsp cornflour (cornstarch)

To serve

Dried beetroot powder (see method, optional)

Chopped pistachios

Finely chopped mint leaves

Add the grated beetroot and maple syrup to a saucepan, place over a low heat and let the syrup bubble away for 15 minutes, until reduced down by about a quarter.

Meanwhile, add the coconut milk to another saucepan with the cardamom pods and vanilla. Place over a low heat and allow the mixture to infuse for 10 minutes.

In a small bowl, whisk together the cashew nut milk and cornflour until smooth.

Whisk the milk mixture into the infused coconut milk mixture, then use a spatula to constantly stir over a low heat until it starts to thicken up.

When the beetroot syrup has reduced down by around a quarter, pass through a sieve (strainer) into the custard mixture, adding enough syrup to achieve a colour and beetroot flavour you like. (The leftover beetroot in the sieve can be dried in a low-temperature oven or dehydrated until crisp, then blitzed in a spice grinder into a vibrant beetroot powder.)

Simmer for 5 minutes, then pass the beetroot custard through a clean sieve into a clean bowl. Cover the surface directly with baking parchment to stop a skin from forming. Allow to cool to room temperature, then place in the fridge until completely chilled.

Add the chilled mixture to an ice-cream machine and let the machine work its magic. Transfer to a freezerproof container and place in the freezer to set properly and enjoy at your leisure.

Serve topped with dried beetroot powder, if you like, chopped pistachios and fresh mint.

Note
Depending on how cool your freezer is, you may have to let your ice cream defrost slightly before serving. You can also add a splash of alcohol (such as rum or vodka) to your custard mix, as since alcohol doesn't freeze, this will help keep your ice cream scoopable.

Marinated Beetroot Carpaccio with Horseradish Cream & Broad Beans

This recipe is an adaptation of a dish I made as a young chef at a restaurant called Le Gallois. At the time, it was a pea soup served with marinated thinly sliced beets and wasabi cream cheese. The best part for me was the beetroots, so I've switched things up to make them the star of the plate. Served with creamy cashew horseradish cream, this is delicious.

SERVES 2 AS LUNCH OR A STARTER

3 uncooked beetroots (beets), peeled

60ml (¼ cup) white wine vinegar or sauerkraut brine

Zest and juice of 1 orange

1 tbsp maple syrup

¼ tsp poppy seeds

Pinch of sea salt

2 tbsp finely chopped chives

3 Szechuan peppercorns, crushed

For the horseradish cream

140g (1 cup/5oz) cashew nuts

250ml (1 cup) boiling water

1 tsp miso paste

3 tbsp white wine vinegar or sauerkraut brine

3 tbsp nutritional yeast

1 tsp wasabi/horseradish purée, or 2 tbsp grated fresh horseradish

4 tbsp extra virgin olive oil

Sea salt

To serve

Broad (fava) beans

Nasturtium leaves

Sourdough or rye bread

Thinly slice the beetroot using a mandoline or sharp knife. In a bowl, whisk together the vinegar or sauerkraut brine with the orange zest and juice, maple syrup, poppy seeds, salt, chives and crushed Szechuan peppercorns. Add the sliced beetroot to the bowl and mix well. Let marinate for at least 30 minutes.

Meanwhile, for the horseradish cream, start by soaking the cashew nuts in the boiling water for about 15 minutes to soften. Once plumped up, drain and transfer the nuts to a blender. Add the miso paste, vinegar or sauerkraut brine, nutritional yeast, and wasabi or horseradish. Blend until smooth, gradually adding the olive oil to achieve a creamy consistency. Season with salt to taste.

To serve, arrange the marinated beetroot slices on a serving plate, drizzling any remaining marinade over the top. Spoon over the horseradish cream and garnish with broad beans, a few peppery nasturtium leaves and some bread.

Pickled Beetroot: Three Ways

I don't pickle things a whole lot any more, because my love for fermentation has taken over; however, you just can't beat pickled beetroot! Here's three different variations using varieties I grow at my home.

FILLS A 2-LITRE (3½-PINT) JAR

5–6 uncooked purple beetroots (beets)

4 tbsp olive oil

3 tsp sea salt

750ml (3 cups) white wine vinegar

250ml (1 cup) water

100g (½ cup/3½oz) caster (superfine) sugar

1 cinnamon stick

3 star anise

6 cloves

2 clementines, halved

1 cardamom pod

2 tsp mustard seeds

1 red onion, finely sliced

1 red chilli, halved

WINTER BY THE FIRE

Preheat your oven to 200°C/180°C fan (400°F/Gas Mark 6).

Peel the beetroots, then cut them into wedges and place on a roasting tray. Drizzle over the olive oil and a little of the salt, then roast for 30 minutes or so, until tender.

Meanwhile, add the vinegar, water, remaining salt, sugar, cinnamon, star anise, cloves, clementines, cardamom, mustard seeds, onion and chilli to a saucepan. Bring to a low simmer for at least 10 minutes, to infuse.

When the beetroot is cooked, carefully add it to the vinegar mixture and let the pickle bubble away for a further 5 minutes before transferring to a sterilized jar.

Once cold, store in the fridge for up to 3 months.

BEETROOT

5–6 uncooked golden
beetroots (beets)

4 tbsp olive oil

3 tsp sea salt

750ml (3 cups) white wine vinegar

250ml (1 cup) water

6 sprigs of thyme

100g (½ cup/3½oz) caster
(superfine) sugar

2 banana shallots, finely sliced

3 garlic cloves, finely sliced

PICKLED GOLDEN BEET & THYME

Preheat your oven to 200°C/180°C fan (400°F/Gas Mark 6).

Peel the beetroots, then cut them into wedges and place on a
roasting tray. Drizzle over the olive oil and a little of the salt,
then roast for 30 minutes or so, until tender.

Bring the vinegar, water, remaining salt, thyme, sugar, shallots
and garlic to a simmer in a large saucepan, simmering for at least
10 minutes, to infuse. Add the cooked beetroot to the pan and leave
to bubble away for 5 minutes before transferring to a sterilized jar.

Once cold, store in the fridge for up to 3 months.

2 tsp sea salt

750ml (3 cups) white wine vinegar

250ml (1 cup) water

1 tsp fennel seeds

Zest of 2 lemons

100g (½ cup/3½oz) caster
(superfine) sugar

1 fennel bulb, finely sliced

5–6 uncooked candy beetroots
(beets), washed and cut into
wedges

CANDY BEET, FENNEL & LEMON PICKLE

This pickle I make a little differently; the beetroot doesn't require
roasting, as I don't want the beautiful pink and white stripes going
brown in the oven. I also don't peel them, as I love the pink skin.

Add everything to a saucepan bar the sliced fennel and beetroot
wedges. Bring the brine to a simmer for 5 minutes, then add the
fennel and beetroot.

Let the beetroot cook away for 15 minutes before transferring
to a sterilized jar.

Once cold, store in the fridge for up to 3 months.

Beet Leaf Curried Kimchi

Beet leaves are so nutritious and earthy, but they're often thrown into the compost heap by most people. Mine are either steamed, fed to my chickens – who absolutely devour them – or turned into this delicious spiced kimchi. Serve it as a side with curries or stews or even in sandwiches.

FILLS A 3-LITRE (5-PINT) JAR

600g (1lb 5oz) beetroot (beet) leaves and stalks, washed and finely chopped

Big handful of coriander (cilantro), roughly chopped

2 carrots, peeled and finely sliced

1 large onion, finely chopped

3 garlic cloves, finely chopped

Thumb-sized piece of ginger, peeled and finely chopped

1 apple, cored and finely chopped

1 tbsp dried chilli flakes (red pepper flakes)

1 tbsp garam masala

Sheet of dried nori seaweed, to seal

Sea salt

Place a large bowl on your weighing scales and set the scale to zero, then add all the ingredients except the nori and salt. Work out what 2% of the weight is, then add that weight in sea salt.

Massage the ingredients together for 5 minutes or so, then cover the bowl with a clean tea (dish) towel and set aside for at least 2 hours so the natural brine is drawn out.

Transfer the mixture, with the brine, to a sterilized jar, leaving 2.5cm (1 inch) of headroom at the top of the jar. Make sure you've added enough brine to cover the mixture by around 1cm (½ inch). Cap the top with the sheet of nori then place a glass fermentation weight on top to hold everything beneath the brine (see page 15 for my fermentation troubleshooting guide). The weight is vital, as if any bits end up floating on the surface of the brine during fermentation, yeast/mould will occur and it could spoil.

Cover loosely with the jar lid or a clean tea towel and leave the kimchi to ferment out of the fridge for about 7 days. Length of fermentation will depend on the temperature of your kitchen. Optimal temperature is around 21°C (70°F). Give the brine a little taste after around the 5-day mark: when it has an acidic tang you like, seal and place it in the fridge, where it can be stored for up to 3 months.

Check the kimchi occasionally to release gas and to look for any signs of yeast on the surface. If you see any, skim it off immediately. The kimchi underneath should still be fine.

Beetroot Peshwari Naan

*Peshwari naans are probably my favourite bread in the whole world.
My version here includes grated homegrown beetroot, which adds the most
exciting vibrant colour when you break into them. I have a unique cooking
technique that will help give the bread a taste not too dissimilar from the
smokiness a tandoor oven provides.*

MAKES 8

350ml (1½ cups) lukewarm water

7g (2 tsp/¼oz) dried fast
action yeast

425g (3 cups/15oz) strong white
bread flour, plus extra for dusting

¼ tsp ground turmeric

2 tsp sea salt

3 tbsp extra virgin olive oil,
plus extra for greasing

4 tbsp raisins

5 tbsp desiccated (dried
shredded) coconut

4 tbsp coconut flour

4 tbsp ground almonds

1 large uncooked beetroot (beet),
peeled and grated

4 tbsp maple syrup

125ml (½ cup) almond milk

Beet leaf curried kimchi (see
page 147), to serve (optional)

In a bowl, mix together the water and yeast and set aside for around
5 minutes until bubbly.

Combine the flour, turmeric and salt in a large bowl or stand mixer.
Make a well in the middle, then add the water and yeast mixture
along with the olive oil. Stir until the mixture starts coming together
into a dough. If using a stand mixer, knead for 5 minutes with the
dough hook attachment. If mixing by hand, turn the dough out
onto a lightly floured work surface and knead for 8 minutes until
the dough is smooth and elastic. Add a little flour while kneading
if you feel it's too sticky. But not too much! Place the dough in a
lightly oiled bowl and cover with a damp tea (dish) towel. Set aside
to rise (double in size) for 1–2 hours.

Meanwhile, for the filling, mix the raisins, coconut, coconut flour,
ground almonds, grated beetroot, maple syrup and almond milk in
a small bowl to form a paste. Set aside until ready to use.

Turn the risen dough out onto a lightly floured work surface and
lightly knead for a minute. Portion into 8 equal-sized pieces and
shape each into a ball. To fill the dough, take one ball of dough
and either stretch with floured hands or roll out into a disc around
5mm (¼ inch) thick. Spread a couple of tablespoons of the coconut
filling onto the centre of the disc, then fold it over itself to encase
the filling within the dough. Roll back out into a naan shape around
5mm (¼ inch) thick and then repeat with the remaining dough balls
and filling.

To cook the naan, for open fire or direct gas-stove cooking, place a
cast-iron pan over a medium-high heat. Add a splash of water to the
pan, then quickly place a naan in the hot pan. Let the naan puff up
slightly and the water evaporate. The water will make the bread stick
to the pan, allowing you to turn the pan upside down, exposing it to
the flame or coals, and allowing you to char the exposed side.

If not cooking over a fire or gas, simply skip the water step and cook
the naans in the dry pan for 3–4 minutes on each side.

When your naans are light, fluffy and a little charred, they're ready.
I like to serve them alongside my beet leaf curried kimchi.

Beetza

For the dough

700g (5 cups/25oz) strong white
bread flour, plus extra for dusting

2 tsp (7g/¼oz) dried fast
action yeast

10g (¼oz) fine sea salt

325ml (1⅓ cups) lukewarm water

125ml (½ cup) beetroot
(beet) juice

60ml (¼ cup) olive oil,
plus extra for greasing

For the rarebit sauce

55g (scant ¼ cup/2oz) olive
oil, plus an extra drizzle for
the topping

1 leek, finely sliced

1 garlic clove, finely sliced

A few sage leaves, finely chopped

35g (¼ cup/1¼oz) plain
(all-purpose) flour

125ml (½ cup) brown ale
(or dark beer of your choice)

2 tsp miso paste

1 tsp English mustard

125ml (½ cup) oat milk

Squeeze of lemon juice

1½ tsp sea salt

1 tsp ground white pepper

15g (¼ cup/½oz) nutritional yeast

For the toppings

6 tbsp beetroot and blackberry
BBQ sauce (see page 139)

Roasted vegetables of your choice

This recipe is a must-try, and brings together my love of pizza, beetroot and the Welsh classic of rarebit – a creamy mustardy sauce that contains jammy leeks and beer. What's not to love? Traditionally, rarebit sauce is used to top toast, but I've found it's a great topping for pizza, especially in partnership with my beetroot and blackberry BBQ sauce (page 139).

For the dough, mix together the flour, yeast and salt in a large bowl or stand mixer. Make a well in the middle, then add the water, beetroot juice and olive oil. Stir or mix until it starts to combine to form a tacky dough.

If using a stand mixer, knead for 6 minutes with the dough hook attachment. If mixing by hand, turn the dough out onto a lightly floured work surface and knead for 8 minutes until the dough is smooth and elastic. Add a little flour while kneading if you feel it's too sticky. But not too much! Place the dough in a lightly oiled bowl and cover with a damp tea (dish) towel. Set aside to rise (double in size) for about 1 hour.

Once the dough has doubled in size, portion it into 6 equal-sized pieces and roll each piece into a ball. Place the dough balls on a lined baking tray, then cover the tray with a damp cloth and let rise somewhere warm for a further 1 hour.

Meanwhile, prepare your rarebit sauce. Place a medium saucepan over a low heat and add the oil. Sauté the leek, garlic and sage for 3–4 minutes until softened. Stir through the flour and cook out for 2 minutes before deglazing the pan with the beer. Cook off the alcohol for a few minutes before stirring through the miso and mustard. Add the milk and whisk or stir until there are no lumps, then stir through the lemon juice and seasoning. Turn the heat to low and let the sauce bubble away for a few minutes to thicken. Fold through the nutritional yeast and remove from the heat.

To cook your beetzas, prepare your pizza oven or preheat your regular oven to its hottest setting.

Roll out the dough balls into rounds about 5mm (¼ inch) thick and spread each with 1 tablespoon of the beet and blackberry BBQ sauce, leaving a 2cm (¾-inch) border around the edge. Top with some roasted vegetables of your choice and dollops of the rarebit sauce, then add a drizzle of olive oil and a sprinkling of salt.

Bake the beetzas in your pizza oven for 2–4 minutes, or on a baking tray in your oven for about 8 minutes, until the dough has puffed up and browned slightly and the rarebit sauce is bubbling.

Beetroot & Chickpea Coconut Curry

SERVES 2-4

4 uncooked beetroots (beets),
cut into bite-sized pieces
(I used candy-striped beets)

For the marinade

250g (1 cup/9oz) coconut yogurt

½ tsp chilli powder

½ tsp ground coriander

½ tsp ground cumin

1 tbsp garam masala

1 tsp ground turmeric

1 green chilli, finely sliced

4 garlic cloves, minced

Zest of ½ lemon

4 tbsp olive oil

1 tsp sea salt

For the curry base

3 tbsp olive oil

1 onion, finely chopped

4 garlic cloves, minced

Thumb-sized piece of fresh
ginger, minced

1 chilli, finely chopped

½ tsp sea salt

1 tsp ground cumin

1 tsp ground coriander

½ tsp ground turmeric

3 tbsp tomato paste

170g (1 cup/6oz) canned or
cooked chickpeas

20g (½ cup/¾oz) toasted
coconut flakes

1 x 400g (14oz) can
of coconut milk

2 big handfuls of baby
spinach leaves

This is another of my dad's recipes – we both really love and are inspired by Indian cuisine. You may not have thought to make a beetroot curry before, but they add a lovely bite, sweetness and earthy flavour among all the spices.

Preheat your oven to 230°C/210°C fan (450°F/Gas Mark 8).

Mix together the marinade ingredients in a large bowl, then stir through the beetroot. Transfer to a baking tray and bake in the oven for 20 minutes, or until the beetroot is tender.

Meanwhile, for the curry base, place a large saucepan over a medium heat and add the olive oil. When hot, add the onion, garlic, ginger and chilli, and cook slowly and gently for around 8 minutes. This will allow the onions to release all their sweetness, adding depth to the curry.

Season with the salt, then add the ground spices. Cook for a further 2 minutes before adding the tomato paste, chickpeas and coconut flakes. Mix well, then add the roasted beetroot.

Deglaze the pan with the coconut milk, stirring well. Let the curry bubble away for 15 minutes, stirring through the spinach just before serving.

Beetroot Fritters with Borscht

SERVES 4

For the borscht

1 tbsp olive oil

1 large onion, finely chopped

4 garlic cloves, finely chopped

2 celery sticks, finely chopped

2 carrots, peeled and grated

Small handful of herbs (I use sage, marjoram and rosemary)

1 tsp celery salt

2 medium uncooked beetroots (beets), washed and grated

2 medium potatoes, peeled and grated

3 tomatoes, roughly chopped

1 litre (4 cups) vegetable stock

1 bay leaf

2 tbsp chopped dill

1 tbsp white wine vinegar

Pinch each of sea salt and black pepper (optional)

For the fritters

2–3 uncooked beetroots (beets), washed and grated

Handful of beetroot leaves, finely shredded

1 onion, finely sliced

3 garlic cloves, minced

Handful of parsley leaves, finely chopped

Handful of dill, finely chopped

1 tsp fennel seeds

Juice of 1 lemon

5 tbsp chickpea (gram) flour

1 tsp sea salt

1 tsp cracked black pepper

1 litre (4 cups) vegetable oil

This is a beetroot overload in a good way! Of course, you don't have to make both the borscht and the fritters, but they really do work nicely in combo! Borscht is an Eastern European staple, and a dish I started making when I sowed way too many beetroots in my garden one year. It's refreshing and rich. The fritters are like pakoras really – crispy, earthy with a hint of fennel seed.

To make the borscht, heat the olive oil in a pan and sweat the onion, garlic, celery and carrots down gently for about 5 minutes with the fresh herbs, seasoning with the celery salt. Add the grated beetroot and potatoes, along with the tomatoes, and cook for a few more minutes before deglazing with the stock. Add the bay leaf, dill, vinegar and additional seasoning if needed. Pop the lid on the pan and let the soup cook for 15 minutes.

Meanwhile, combine all the fritter ingredients except the vegetable oil in a bowl and stir well. Add a little water if needed to help everything bind.

Heat the vegetable oil in a heavy-based skillet or large saucepan (ensuring the oil comes no further than halfway up the sides of the pan) set over a medium heat. Bring it to about 180°C (356°F). To test if the oil is hot enough, place a wooden spoon in the pan; if bubbles form around the spoon, it is hot enough to fry. Add spoonfuls of the fritter mixture to the hot oil and fry for around 5 minutes, flipping over halfway through, until crispy and a little golden. Remove to a plate lined with kitchen paper to soak up any excess oil.

Serve the borscht in bowls with a few crispy fritters for dipping.

chilli

Chilli Sambal with BBQ Runner Beans

I first tried sambal in Indonesia. It has everything: sweetness, spiciness and saltiness. It's a great way to make use of all my homegrown chillies. Spread over my charred runner beans, it creates a deliciously simple spicy garden snack.

SERVES 4–6 AS A SIDE

1kg (2lb 3oz) runner beans, trimmed

Sea salt

For the sambal

10 mild red chillies

3 hot red chillies

Olive oil, for cooking

1 white onion, roughly chopped

4 garlic cloves, peeled

1 large tomato, quartered

4 tbsp fermented bean curd (from a can) or 4 tbsp light soy sauce

1 tbsp miso paste

50g (⅓ cup/1¾oz) coconut sugar

3 tbsp rice wine vinegar

To garnish

Crispy onions

Toasted sesame seeds

Chopped spring onions (scallions)

Before making the sambal, I like to grill my chillies over hot coals on my BBQ, until lightly charred and tender, but a cast-iron pan over a high heat will also do.

Add a little oil to a pan over a medium heat, then add the onion, garlic and tomato. Sauté for 4–5 minutes or until caramelized. Transfer to a food processor along with the charred chillies, fermented bean curd or soy, miso, coconut sugar, rice wine vinegar and a pinch of salt. Blitz the mixture until smooth. The sambal can be stored in a sealed container in the fridge for up to 2 weeks and can be added to stir-fries, ramen broths or anything that needs a bit of heat.

Toss the runner beans with 1 teaspoon of salt, then BBQ them over an intense heat until tender and blackened in places. When cooked, pile the beans onto a serving dish and top with lots of sambal, some crispy onions, sesame seeds and spring onions.

Dried Chilli Spice Mix
with Celeriac Crisps

A good way to preserve your homegrown chilli harvest – or a bunch of chillies from your local store – is to dry them. Once they're dried, you can simply store them in jars ready to put in soups, sauces and stews. But you could also make your own signature chilli spice blend, unique to you, to season up some of your favourite dishes, preserving the flavour of your crop and adding life to dishes for months to come. In fact, a properly dried spice blend can last over a year. I dry my chillies in my dehydrator but a low-temperature oven will also work; just dry them until they're totally crisp, as there cannot be any moisture left inside. Below is one of my favourite spice blends and a unique way of using it on crispy celeriac. I like using a small celeriac here so I can slice it whole on a mandoline.

FILLS 1 SMALL JAR

For the spice mix

3 tbsp cumin seeds

2 tbsp fennel seeds

2 tbsp coriander seeds

50g (½ cup/1¾oz) dried chilli flakes (red pepper flakes)

3 tbsp garlic granules

3 tbsp onion granules

2 tbsp celery salt

For the celeriac crisps

1 small celeriac (celery root)

1 litre (4 cups) vegetable oil

For the spice mix, place a small frying pan over a low heat and, when hot, add the cumin, fennel and coriander seeds. Toast for about 3 minutes, then allow them to cool before grinding them in a spice grinder or powerful blender with the chilli flakes, garlic and onion granules, and the celery salt.

The spice mix should last well over 6 months but the flavour will drop off the longer you keep it.

For the celeriac crisps, line a large tray with a clean tea (dish) towel.

Peel your celeriac with a sharp knife or potato peeler, then use a mandoline to slice it super fine.

Heat the oil in a heavy-based skillet or large saucepan (ensuring the oil comes no further than halfway up the sides of the pan) set over a medium heat. Bring it to about 180°C (356°F). To test if the oil is hot enough, place a wooden spoon in the pan; if bubbles form around the spoon, it is hot enough to fry.

Add the celeriac slices in batches to the hot oil and fry until crisp and golden. Remove them to a plate lined with kitchen paper to soak up any excess oil. At this stage you can optionally refry them in the oil, to achieve an even crispier texture.

Add the freshly fried crisps to a bowl along with 1–2 tablespoons of the spice mix and toss well to coat.

My Dad's Crunchy Chilli Oil

Chinese-style crunchy chilli oil is good on pretty much everything and my Dad's recipe is one of my favourite versions. Packed with crispy, crunchy texture and with a hit of dried homegrown chilli heat, I assure you a jar of this won't be around for long.

FILLS 2 X 350ML (12OZ) JARS

500ml (2 cups) flavourless oil, such as sunflower

5 garlic cloves, peeled

¼ white onion

2 cardamom pods, bashed

Thumb-sized piece of ginger, peeled and minced

150g (1½ cups/5½oz) dried chilli flakes (red pepper flakes)

1 tbsp garlic granules or crispy garlic flakes

1 heaped tbsp crispy onions

1 tbsp fermented black soy beans, finely chopped, or use miso paste

1 tbsp brown sugar

2 tsp sea salt

In a small saucepan, heat the oil gently with the garlic, onion and cardamom pods over a low heat. Leave to infuse for 5 minutes, then remove from the heat.

Meanwhile, add the remaining ingredients to a heatproof bowl and stir well, then set a sieve (strainer) above the bowl. When the oil has infused and is still hot, pour it through the sieve into the bowl to remove the garlic, onion and cardamom. Discard the contents of the sieve and stir everything really well.

Once cooled, transfer the chilli oil to a sterilized jar and store it at room temperature. Eat within 1 month.

Fermented Chilli Cucumber Spirals

We all know and love dill pickles. Well, this is a twist on that – literally. Cucumbers cut into spirals and fermented with chilli become tangy and super savoury. Serve them simply with rice or as a side.

FILLS A 3-LITRE (5-PINT) JAR

At least 6 small cucumbers

3 tbsp dried nori seaweed flakes, or 1 blitzed sheet of dried nori

3 tbsp light soy sauce

Sea salt

Per cucumber:

¼ hot chilli, very finely chopped

½ spring onion (scallion), very finely chopped

½ garlic clove

1 bay leaf

½ tsp minced fresh ginger

1 tsp toasted sesame seeds

First up, let's turn the cucumbers into spirals. Place a cucumber lengthways between 2 chopsticks (they act as a guide to stop you from cutting all the way through). Using a sharp knife, make diagonal cuts across the cucumber, slicing down until the knife hits the chopsticks. Once you've cut the entire length of the cucumber on one side, flip it over and make similar diagonal cuts on the opposite side, this time in the opposite direction. Repeat with all your cucumbers.

Place a large bowl on your weighing scales and set it to zero. Add the cucumbers to the bowl along with the seaweed flakes and soy sauce, adding the appropriate amount of chilli, spring onion, garlic, bay leaves, ginger and sesame seeds.

Take the weight of the contents and work out what 3% of that weight is. Weigh out that amount in sea salt and sprinkle it over the cucumbers. Use your hands to gently mix everything up, trying not to break up the spirals. Cover the bowl and set aside for at least 4 hours, for liquid to be drawn out.

Transfer the cucumbers, with the brine, to a large sterilized jar, leaving 2.5cm (1 inch) of headroom at the top of the jar. Make sure you've added enough brine to cover the mixture by around 1cm (½ inch). Place a glass fermentation weight on top to hold the cucumbers beneath the brine (see page 15 for my fermentation troubleshooting guide).

Seal the jar and leave somewhere dark and warm to ferment for up to 10 days. The speed of fermentation depends on the temperature in your kitchen; the warmer it is, the faster it is. Every now and then during fermentation, open the jar to release any gas that may have built up (unless using an airlock where the gas is naturally released).

When the brine is tangy and quite acidic, transfer the jar to the fridge to slow the fermentation down. If submerged in the brine the whole time, the cucumbers should keep for up to 3 months.

Salted Chilli & Olive Oil Chocolate Mousse with Toasted Hazelnuts

Super creamy, chocolatey and with a hint of chilli, this is a decadent dessert that is much easier to whip up than you'd think. If you serve it with chilli oil (see page 164), be sure to make a batch without the onion, garlic and soy beans.

SERVES 4-6

60ml (¼ cup) extra virgin olive oil, plus a little extra to finish

1 dried ancho chilli

4 dried árbol chillies

250g (1½ cups/9oz) dark (bittersweet) chocolate, finely chopped

2 x 300g (10½oz) blocks of silken tofu, drained

1 tbsp vanilla bean paste

60ml (¼ cup) maple syrup

½ tsp sea salt flakes, plus a little extra to finish

4 tbsp cacao powder

125ml (½ cup) liquid from a can of chickpeas (aquafaba)

1 tbsp icing (confectioners') sugar

50g (½ cup/1¾oz) toasted hazelnuts, roughly chopped

Your favourite chill oil, to serve (optional)

First, combine the olive oil with the chillies in a heatproof bowl. Grab a saucepan big enough for the bottom of the bowl to sit about 5cm (2 inches) from the bottom of the pan, then add a 2.5cm (1-inch) depth of water to the pan.

Sit the bowl on top of the pan, then place over a low heat. Allow the chillies to infuse for about 15 minutes. Keep an eye on the oil to ensure it remains warm but not hot.

Add the chocolate directly into the infused oil. Stir gently as the chocolate begins to melt, allowing it to combine smoothly with the infused chilli oil. Once the chocolate is fully melted and silky, remove and discard the chillies. Take the bowl off the pan and set it aside to cool slightly.

Add the silken tofu, vanilla bean paste, maple syrup and salt to a blender. Blend until the mixture becomes completely smooth and creamy, then add the cacao powder and blend again. With the mixer running on a very low speed, gradually pour in the chilli-infused oil and chocolate mixture, until it comes together. Transfer the mixture to a clean bowl.

Add the chickpea liquid and icing sugar to a separate, large bowl. Using an electric mixer, whip the liquid on a medium to high speed until it forms stiff peaks and is fluffy and light, similar to whipped meringue. This can take 5–10 minutes.

Add a few heaped spoonfuls of the whipped aquafaba to the chocolate mixture and fold it in carefully to lighten the mix. Then, in batches, gently fold the remaining whipped aquafaba through the chocolate mixture to create an even lighter consistency, until it is all mixed through. Transfer the mousse to the fridge to cool and firm up slightly.

To serve, spoon the mousse onto plates and finish with some hazelnuts, a drizzle of olive oil and some flaky sea salt. If you're feeling adventurous you can also serve this with a drizzle of chilli oil.

Scotch Bonnet Black Bean Patties & Scotch Bonnet Jam

MAKES 8

For the pastry

425g (3 cups/15oz) spelt flour, plus extra for dusting

1½ tsp fine sea salt

1 tsp curry powder

225g (1 cup/8oz) cold butter, cubed

2 tbsp white wine vinegar

2 tbsp ice-cold water, plus more if needed

For the filling

1 tablespoon olive oil

6 spring onions (scallions), finely chopped

4 garlic cloves, minced

1 Scotch bonnet chilli, deseeded and finely chopped

1 tsp ground cumin

1 tsp ground allspice

½ tsp ground cinnamon

3 tbsp thyme leaves

3 tbsp tomato paste

440g (2 cups/15½oz) canned or cooked black beans

1 tbsp miso paste (or coconut aminos for soy free)

125ml (½ cup) vegetable stock

1 tsp sea salt

250g (8 cups/9oz) baby spinach or fresh callaloo leaves

For the glaze

2 tbsp maple syrup

3 tbsp olive oil

During my time in Jamaica, I must have eaten my body weight in patties, or, as my Rasta friend Vita calls them, yatties. Crisp, flaky pastry packed with an array of delicious fillings, these patties are loosely inspired by those I had on my favourite island, using Scotch bonnet chillies I grew in my greenhouse. They are a staple in Caribbean cuisine, and now also in my kitchen. They aren't just hot, they're aromatic, and they grow on the plant like little lanterns of red, gold and green. I serve these delicious spelt patties with spicy chilli jam, too.

For the pastry, combine the flour with the salt and curry powder in a large bowl. Add the cold, cubed butter and work it in with your fingers until it has a breadcrumb-like consistency.

Add the vinegar and water and mix just until the dough begins to come together (add more water if needed). Once the dough has formed, shape it into a disc, wrap and chill in the fridge while you make the filling.

Heat the olive oil in a large pan over a medium heat. Add the spring onions and cook until they soften. Stir in the garlic and chilli and allow to cook for a minute or two to release their flavours. Sprinkle in the ground spices and thyme, and cook them out for 2 minutes.

Next, stir in the tomato paste and black beans, coating them well in all the flavours. Whisk the miso paste into the stock, then deglaze the pan with it, scraping the bottom of the pan with a wooden spoon to release some of that goodness that may be on the bottom. Season with the salt, then let the mix bubble away for 20 minutes, giving the beans a light mash with a fork as they're cooking. When the liquid has reduced down, stir through the spinach or callaloo. Remove from the heat and let the filling cool completely.

Preheat your oven to 200°C/180°C fan (400°F/Gas Mark 6). Line a flat baking tray with baking parchment.

Whisk together the glaze ingredients in a small bowl.

Continued...

Roll out the dough on a lightly floured surface to about 5mm (¼ inch) thick, then cut out 8 circles around 15cm (6 inches) in diameter (you may find it easier to cut out 4 circles, then gather and reroll the dough to cut out another 4 circles). Spoon a few tablespoons of the cooled filling onto one half of each circle, brush the edges with a little glaze and then fold the other half over to encase the filling. Press the edges together to seal, then crimp the edges with a fork to ensure the patties are well sealed. Place on your lined baking tray and brush the rest of the glaze over the top, then use a small knife to make a slit in the top of each patty to allow some steam to escape while they bake

Bake the patties in the oven for 45 minutes or until the pastry is golden brown and crisp. Serve with Scotch bonnet chilli jam (see below).

1 onion, roughly chopped

1 garlic bulb, cloves peeled

3 tbsp minced fresh ginger

6 Scotch bonnet chillies, deseeded

4 red (bell) peppers, deseeded

2 tbsp tomato paste

250ml (1 cup) white wine vinegar

200g (1 cup/7oz) caster (superfine) sugar

SCOTCH BONNET CHILLI JAM

Add the onion, garlic, ginger, chillies and peppers to a food processor and blitz until finely chopped.

Add to a saucepan with the remaining ingredients, stir really well and then place the pan over a low heat. Let the mix bubble away for 35–40 minutes, stirring every now and then.

It is ready when it has turned jammy and rather sticky. Allow the jam to cool completely before transferring to sterilized jars. It will store in the fridge for a couple of months.

Pear, Fig, Rosemary & Chilli Tarte Tatin

Tarte tatin has always been one of my favourite desserts, and unveiling it at the table adds a wow factor to your dinners. I love the fine balance of sweet and savoury in this version. All these ingredients in my garden are harvestable at a similar time believe it or not – my chillies take a long time to ripen in my greenhouse, so I often pick them in October with pears and figs. It's important that you use a 23–25cm (9–10 inches) heavy-bottomed non-stick frying pan that is also ovenproof for this recipe.

SERVES 6-8

1 sheet ready-rolled puff pastry (or use homemade rough-puff, see below)

150g (¾ cup/5½oz) butter

1 hot red chilli, such as habanero or Scotch bonnet, halved

2 sprigs of rosemary

150g (¾ cup/5½oz) light brown sugar, plus extra to finish

8 pears, peeled, cored and halved

5 figs, halved

½ tsp ground cinnamon

For the pastry

425g (3 cups/15oz) plain (all-purpose) flour, plus extra for dusting

Pinch of salt

½ tsp ground cinnamon

3 tbsp caster (superfine) sugar

225g (1 cup/8oz) cold butter, cubed

About 2 tbsp cold milk

To serve

Ice cream (see page 140 for homemade)

Dried chilli (red pepper) flakes

Preheat your oven to 220°C/200°C fan (425°F/Gas Mark 7).

If making your own pastry, combine the dry ingredients in a large bowl. Add the butter and work it in with your fingers until it has a breadcrumb-like consistency. Add the milk and mix just until the dough comes together (add more milk if needed). Once the dough has formed, shape it into a disc, wrap and chill in the fridge for 20 minutes.

On a sheet of lightly floured baking parchment, roll and cut the pastry into a rough circle the same diameter as your pan (see the recipe introduction); it doesn't have to be super neat. Place a cloth over the pastry while you prepare the filling.

Heat the pan over a low heat and add the butter, chilli and rosemary and let them infuse into the butter for 2–3 minutes, without letting the butter burn. Add the sugar and allow to melt down into a golden caramel, letting the heat do the work and trying not to stir it. Now start placing the fruit in the pan, slightly overlapping, and mostly cut side down. Pack the pan as tightly as you can, as the fruit will shrink.

Sprinkle over a dusting of extra sugar and the cinnamon, then carefully lay the pastry on top of the pan, using the baking parchment to help you lift it. Quickly and carefully tuck the pastry down right into the edges, using a wooden spoon so you don't have to touch the hot pan. Prick the pastry a few times with a fork or knife, then bake in the oven for 30–35 minutes or until the pastry is golden and crisp.

Remove the tart from the oven and allow it to cool for 5 minutes before placing your serving board or plate on top of the pan (make sure it's larger than the pan). Put an oven glove on to protect the arm holding the board (some caramel goodness may drip out and it's super hot), then quickly, carefully and confidently turn it out.

Serve with ice cream and a sprinkle of dried chilli flakes.

Shiitake Chilli Hot Pot

When I say that this is a hot pot, I really mean it! It's warming and fiery, this time thanks to homegrown jalapeños – although you can use whatever spicy chillies you have to hand. Just make sure you take time to toast the spices in the hot oil and allow the mushrooms to cook down and caramelize. Topped with crispy potato, this is the perfect dish on a cold day.

SERVES 4

60ml (¼ cup) olive oil

1 large onion, finely chopped

5 garlic cloves, minced

1 mild jalapeño chilli, finely sliced

2 tsp mild chilli powder

2 tsp sweet smoked paprika
or ¼ tsp hot smoked paprika

1 tsp ground cumin

1 tsp fennel seeds

1 tbsp dried oregano

2 tbsp tomato paste

600g (21oz) shiitake mushrooms

1 x 400g (14oz) can of red
kidney beans

1 bay leaf

1 cinnamon stick

2 tsp sea salt

4 tbsp light soy sauce

For the topping and garnish

1 large potato (I use Maris
Piper), peeled

Olive oil, for drizzling

Pinch of sea salt

Sliced green chilli (optional)

Begin by heating the olive oil in a large ovenproof casserole dish over a medium heat. Add the onion, allowing it to soften and become caramelized, stirring occasionally to prevent it from browning too quickly. Once the onion is golden, add the garlic and sliced chilli, cooking for a couple of minutes.

Next, stir in the chilli powder, paprika, cumin, fennel seeds and oregano, allowing the spices to toast a little in the hot oil. Add the tomato paste, stirring it into the mixture until it begins to darken slightly.

Toss in the shiitake mushrooms, stirring them through the fiery mixture. Allow them to cook down slowly, absorbing all the flavours. They will release their moisture at first, but continue to cook them until the moisture evaporates and they start to brown.

When the shiitakes have caramelized, add the kidney beans (and liquid from the can), bay leaf, cinnamon stick, salt and soy sauce. Stir it all together, making sure everything's coated, then let the mixture simmer away gently for about 15 minutes over a low heat.

Meanwhile, preheat your oven to 220°C/200°C fan (425°F/Gas Mark 7) and prepare the potato topping. Slice the potato to around 2mm (¹⁄₁₆ inch) thick, using a mandoline or a sharp knife.

Remove the bay leaf and cinnamon stick from the casserole dish, then arrange the sliced potato on top of the filling, overlapping each piece. Drizzle with a little olive oil, sprinkle with a little salt and transfer to the oven for 35 minutes or until the potatoes are crisp and golden brown. Scatter with sliced green chilli to serve, if you like.

Fire Cider

Believe it or not, for me this is the most important recipe in the entire book… Fire cider is a traditional herbal remedy used for centuries. It uses fiery ingredients, from my homegrown chillies to ginger, garlic and turmeric. Raw apple cider vinegar extracts the goodness from each ingredient, making it a potent remedy for colds, and boosting your immune system. Not only that, but it tastes delicious, and you can use it in simple salad dressings for a potent kick. I take a tablespoon of fire cider every day during the winter, mixed into a small glass of water.

MAKES 1 LARGE JAR

5 hot chillies, such as jalapeño or Scotch bonnet, quartered

2 onions, roughly chopped

3 garlic bulbs, halved horizontally

50g (½ cup/2oz) roughly chopped fresh ginger

50g (½ cup/2oz) roughly chopped fresh turmeric root

2 lemons, cut into chunks

5g (¼ cup/¼oz) rosemary sprigs

5g (¼ cup/¼oz) sage leaves

1 cinnamon stick

3 star anise

3 cloves

1 tbsp black peppercorns

3 tbsp dried elderberries (optional)

1.5 litres (6 cups) raw apple cider vinegar

Maple syrup, to sweeten (optional)

Add all the solid ingredients to a large, sealable sterilized jar, then pour over the apple cider vinegar to cover completely.

Store the jar in a cool, dark place for about 3–4 weeks, shaking the jar every few days to agitate the mixture.

After the steeping period, strain the liquid through a fine-mesh sieve (strainer) or cheesecloth into a sterilized glass container. Squeeze out as much liquid as possible.

You can sweeten your fire cider with maple syrup to taste if you find it too strong: start with a tablespoon and adjust from there.

Store the fire cider in the fridge, where it will keep for several months, or even longer.

Take 1–2 tablespoons daily, mixed with water.

Note
To turn the fire cider into a lovely salad dressing, simply whisk it in a bowl with equal parts olive oil, tahini and maple syrup.

After infusing, the strained ingredients can be dehydrated and turned into a seasoning powder (or composted!).

Fermented Chilli Hot Sauce

Forget all you know about standard hot sauces – fermented hot sauce is on another level. I actually grow chillies just to make this hot sauce. During the fermentation process the chillies lose a lot of their heat and become more fruity and tangy. I use the sauce as a seasoning too, as it's got so much umami.

MAKES 1 LITRE (2 PINTS)

1 large onion

300g (10½oz) fresh chillies (I use a mixture of varieties from my greenhouse)

4 red (bell) peppers, halved and deseeded

1 garlic bulb, cloves peeled and crushed

Spring water, to cover

Sea salt

4 tbsp caster (superfine) sugar

Slice a side of the onion off to use a layer as the kimchi 'plug', then roughly chop the rest of the onion and add it to a large bowl with the chillies, peppers and garlic. Mix well to combine.

Place a large sterilized jar on your weighing scales and set it to zero. Add the chilli mixture to the jar. Pour over enough spring water to cover the ingredients by around 2cm (¾ inch), leaving at least 4cm (1½ inches) of headroom below the top. Work out what 2% of the combined weight is, then add that weight in sea salt and the 4 tablespoons of sugar.

Seal tightly and give the jar a good shake to dissolve the salt and sugar, then unseal the lid. Place the reserved piece of onion over the top to 'plug' the ingredients beneath the brine, then place a fermentation weight on top, to hold everything beneath (see page 15 for my fermentation troubleshooting guide). It's important you don't have any ingredients floating on the top of the brine, as this could cause a mould/yeast to form on the surface.

Reseal the jar and leave to ferment for 3–4 weeks; the warmer the temperature in your house, the quicker the fermentation, but with whole chillies it's likely it will take slightly longer. During the fermentation, the chilli will mellow in heat and also soften, as the acidity generated almost 'cooks' the contents of the jar. 'Burp' the jar every couple of days, to release any build-up of gas.

After 3 weeks, taste the brine and, when it's tangy and rather acidic, transfer the contents of the jar (except the brine) to a blender and blitz until super smooth. Now add a little of the brine and blend again – you want to add just enough of the brine to create a smooth, velvety sauce. If your blender isn't super powerful, I recommend passing the sauce through a sieve (strainer).

Transfer the sauce to sterilized bottles and store in the fridge for up to 3 months. It will naturally separate, so just shake before using.

onion

Burnt Onion Hummus with Crispy Onions

If you love hummus, then this is a great way to level it up. The burnt onions add a jammy, smoky dimension to this dip that is hard to resist. I like to blend my hummus super smooth, but you can blend it to whatever consistency you prefer.

SERVES 4

For the hummus

340g (2 cups/12oz) dried chickpeas

2 tsp sea salt, plus extra to taste

4 onions

6 tbsp tahini

4 garlic cloves, peeled

2 tsp cumin seeds, toasted

Juice of 1 lemon

4 tbsp olive oil

For the crispy onions

500ml (2 cups) neutral oil

2 onions, very finely sliced

To garnish

Extra virgin olive oil

Sumac

Place the dried chickpeas in a bowl and add cold water to cover by about 2.5cm (1 inch). Leave to soak overnight.

The next day, drain and rinse them, place in a large saucepan, cover with fresh water and add the salt. Bring to the boil, then reduce the heat and allow them to simmer until tender, around 1 hour.

While the chickpeas are cooking, start your BBQ or wood fire and burn until you have white coals. Place the whole onions directly in the coals and allow the skins to blacken. This smokiness will penetrate through the layers and the insides will slowly cook. (This can also be done in a conventional oven, but nothing beats the smokiness of an open fire.) Once the onions are blackened, set them aside to cool a little.

When the chickpeas are cooked, transfer them to a blender (reserving a few for garnish) with around 250ml (1 cup) of their cooking water, the tahini, garlic, cumin seeds and lemon juice. Blitz until super smooth, adding a little extra liquid if you need too, along with extra salt to taste. Scrape the hummus into a large bowl.

Once cool enough to handle, peel and discard the blackened skin from the onions and add the flesh to the blender (no need to clean it). Add the olive oil and blitz until puréed. Fold the burnt onion purée through the hummus until just combined, reserving a little onion purée for topping.

To make the crispy onions, heat the oil in a heavy-based skillet or large saucepan (ensuring the oil comes no further than halfway up the sides of the pan) set over a medium heat. Bring it to about 180°C (356°F). To test if the oil is hot enough, place a wooden spoon in the pan; if bubbles form around the spoon, it is hot enough to fry. Add the sliced onions and a pinch of salt to the oil and fry until golden and crisp. Using a slotted spoon, remove the onions to a plate lined with kitchen paper to soak up any excess oil.

Serve up the hummus topped with the reserved chickpeas and burnt onion purée, extra virgin olive oil, the crispy onions and a sprinkling of sumac.

Caramelized Onions

The perfect way to prepare and store a glut, these caramelized onions will keep for months in the fridge and can be used as a base for soups or stews, spread on toast, or in delicious dishes like my cornbread, overleaf. If you wish to make a smaller batch, do simply halve the quantities given here.

MAKES ENOUGH TO FILL ABOUT 4 SMALL JARS

3kg (6lb 10oz) onions

5 tbsp olive oil

250ml (1 cup) cider (hard cider) or apple juice

80ml (⅓ cup) apple cider vinegar

230g (1 cup/8oz) soft brown sugar or coconut sugar

1 tbsp sea salt

1 tbsp thyme leaves

First up, peel, halve, then thinly slice all the onions; you may need goggles for this, but it'll be worth it.

Heat a large, heavy-based pan over a medium heat and add the olive oil. When hot, add the onions. Now you have to be patient. Let the onions cook away really slowly, stirring every now and then. The longer you allow them to cook, the sweeter they become; I'd allow 25 minutes. Adjust the temperature if you feel the onions are catching on the bottom, as you don't want them to burn.

When the onions have cooked down and turned golden brown, pour in the cider or apple juice, stirring to deglaze the pan and loosen any delicious bits stuck to the bottom. Let the liquid reduce slightly before adding the apple cider vinegar, sugar, salt and thyme.

Leave to cook down over a low heat for around 30 minutes, stirring every now and then; you want the liquid to thicken up to a syrupy consistency.

When the liquid is sticky and the onions are really caramelized, remove from the heat and leave to cool. When cool, transfer to sterilized jars and store in the fridge for up to 3 months.

Caramelized Onion Cornbread

Cornbread is hugely popular all over the world nowadays, and I find it so versatile in terms of the amount of flavours you can incorporate. It originated from Native American cuisine, where corn is a staple. I grow corn in my garden but I'm yet to dry it and turn it into cornmeal! This cornbread is deliciously flavoured with caramelized onions and fennel seeds.

SERVES 8

340g (2 cups/12oz) fine polenta (cornmeal)

280g (2 cups/10oz) plain (all-purpose) flour

2 tsp baking powder

2 tsp bicarbonate of soda (baking soda)

1 tsp sea salt

500ml (2 cups) milk

125ml (½ cup) olive oil

120ml (½ cup) maple syrup

60ml (¼ cup) apple cider vinegar

1 tbsp fennel seeds, toasted

2 tbsp chia seeds

250g (1 cup/9oz) caramelized onions (see page 189)

Butter, to serve (optional)

Relish of your choice, to serve (I like it with my strawberry and hibiscus chutney on page 40)

Preheat your oven to 220°C/200°C fan (425°F/Gas Mark 7). Grease a 20cm (8-inch) cast-iron skillet.

In a large bowl, combine the polenta, flour, baking powder, bicarb and salt. Whisk together until well combined.

In another bowl, mix the milk, olive oil, maple syrup, apple cider vinegar, fennel seeds, chia seeds and half the caramelized onions, and stir until well combined.

Pour the wet ingredients into the dry ingredients and fold the two together until just combined.

Pour the batter into the prepared skillet, then use your hands to drop clumps of the remaining caramelized onions into the batter. Do this really randomly; it's supposed to be rustic.

Bake in the oven for 40–45 minutes, or until the top is golden and a toothpick inserted into the centre comes out clean (if the top is browning too much before the cornbread is baked through, simply cover with a sheet of foil).

Leave to cool for 20 minutes in the tin or skillet (dot with extra butter, if you like) before slicing and serving with some relish.

Fermented Onion & Sultana Pakoras

'Quick fermenting' onions with garlic, ginger and spices adds a tang to these crispy pakoras that you'll really enjoy. I know it's a two-day wait for the deliciousness, but it is worth it, I promise. The brine that is created adds depth and a little saltiness to the yogurt dip, making it the perfect accompaniment to the pakoras.

SERVES 4-6

1 tsp mustard seeds

1 tsp cumin seeds

1 tsp fennel seeds

1 tsp caraway seeds

3 onions, finely sliced

1 tbsp minced fresh ginger

5 garlic cloves, minced

1 red chilli, finely chopped

Handful of coriander (cilantro), finely chopped

50g (½ cup/1¾oz) sultanas (golden raisins)

1 tsp nigella seeds

70g (½ cup/2½oz) chickpea (gram) flour

1 litre (4 cups) neutral oil, for frying

Sea salt

For the tangy yogurt dip

120g (1 cup/4oz) coconut yogurt

75g (2½oz) cucumber, chopped into small cubes

1 tbsp finely chopped mint leaves

1 garlic clove, minced

1 green chilli, finely chopped

Place a small frying pan over a low heat. When hot, toast the spices for a couple of minutes, or until you can smell their fragrance. Remove from the pan and set aside.

Add the sliced onions to a large bowl, along with the ginger, garlic, chilli and all the toasted spices.

Weigh the contents of the bowl and add 1% of that weight in sea salt. Mix everything up really well, then cover the bowl and leave it somewhere warm to ferment for 48 hours. Stir the mixture once or twice during fermentation.

Once fermented, drain the liquid from the onions, reserving it for the dressing.

Into the bowl with the onions, add the coriander, sultanas, nigella seeds and chickpea flour. Mix really well, until everything sticks together (add a splash of fermenting brine if needed). Set aside until you're ready to fry.

Make the tangy yogurt dip by simply mixing the reserved brine with the remaining dip ingredients.

To fry the pakoras, heat the oil in a heavy-based skillet or large saucepan (ensuring the oil comes no further than halfway up the sides of the pan) set over a medium heat. Bring it to about 180°C (356°F). To test if the oil is hot enough, place a wooden spoon in the pan; if bubbles form around the spoon, it is hot enough to fry.

Spoon dollops of the onion batter carefully into the hot oil and fry for around 4–5 minutes, adjusting the heat if the pakoras are colouring too fast, and turning them over as they fry so they cook and colour evenly. Remove to a plate lined with kitchen paper to absorb any excess oil, and continue frying until you have used all the batter.

Serve the pakoras with lots of the tangy yogurt dip.

Pickled Little Onions

I often have the joy of harvesting some giant onions, but sometimes many are on the small side, and these I tend to pickle. Pickled onions are a classic in the UK, and making them at home couldn't be easier. It's a great way to use those small onions and preserve the harvest for longer.

FILLS A 1-LITRE (2-PINT) JAR

1kg (2lb 3oz) small or baby onions, peeled

100g (3½oz) sea salt

750ml (3 cups) malt vinegar

200g (7oz) maple syrup

1 dried chilli

2 tsp mustard seeds

2 bay leaves

Start by placing the peeled onions in a large bowl and sprinkling over the salt. Toss the onions to coat them evenly, then cover the bowl and let it sit at room temperature overnight.

The next day, rinse the onions thoroughly under cold water to remove the excess salt, then drain and set aside while you prepare the pickling brine.

In a saucepan, combine the vinegar, maple syrup, chilli, mustard seeds and bay leaves. Bring the mixture to a simmer over a medium heat, stirring every now and then, then let it simmer for 5–6 minutes to allow the spices to infuse. Remove from the heat.

Pack the onions into a sterilized jar, ensuring they are tightly packed in. Pour the hot vinegar mixture over the onions, making sure the liquid covers them completely.

Seal the jar with an airtight lid and allow to cool to room temperature before transferring to the fridge. Allow at least 2 weeks before tasting.

The pickled onions will keep for up to 6 months and can be enjoyed with so many dishes.

Sticky Onion, Celeriac & Chestnut Galette

I love making galettes because the pastry is very forgiving. Actually, the more rustic the pastry is, the better it looks. So don't worry if the pastry tears or breaks – just patch it up! It's packed with lovely seeds, and the filling is hearty, oniony and warming.

SERVES 4-6

6 small onions, peeled and halved

1 small celeriac (celery root), peeled and cut into wedges

180g (6½oz) vacuum-packed cooked chestnuts

3 tbsp olive oil, plus extra to serve

3 tbsp pomegranate molasses or maple syrup

4 tbsp red wine vinegar

2 tbsp wholegrain mustard

1 tbsp miso paste

8 thyme sprigs, plus extra leaves to garnish

For the pastry

140g (1 cup/5oz) buckwheat flour

140g (1 cup/5oz) spelt flour (or replace with more buckwheat flour for gluten-free)

Pinch of sea salt

120g (½ cup/4oz) cold butter, cubed

2 tbsp olive oil

About 5 tbsp ice-cold water

2 tbsp pumpkin seeds

2 tbsp flax seeds

1 tbsp sunflower seeds

1 tbsp sesame seeds

Preheat your oven to 200°C/180°C fan (400°F/Gas Mark 6).

For the pastry, in a bowl, mix together the buckwheat flour, spelt flour and salt. Add the cold butter cubes and olive oil and rub them into the flour mixture until it has a breadcrumb-like consistency.

Stir in just enough cold water for the dough to come together. Add all the seeds, kneading them until they are evenly distributed throughout the dough. Form the dough into a ball, then cover the bowl and let it rest in the fridge while you make the filling.

For the filling, add the onions, celeriac wedges and chestnuts to a baking dish. In a small bowl, whisk together the olive oil, pomegranate molasses or maple syrup, the vinegar, mustard, miso and thyme until smooth. Pour this over the onion mixture and mix really well, making sure everything is coated.

Bake in the oven for 45 minutes or until the liquid becomes sticky and the vegetables are tender. Remove and allow to cool to room temperature.

Roll out the chilled dough on a floured sheet of baking parchment into a rough circle about 5mm (¼ inch) thick. The pastry may break up, but this is a rustic dish so don't worry if you have to patch areas up. Spoon the onion, celeriac and chestnut mixture into the centre of the pastry, leaving a clear border around the edges. Fold the edges of the pastry up over the filling, leaving the centre exposed. Slide the parchment and pastry onto a baking sheet.

Place the galette in the oven and bake for 25 minutes, or until the pastry is golden and crisp. Serve garnished with a sprinkling of thyme and a drizzle of olive oil.

Stuffed Harissa Onions

I had a stuffed onion dish at the Casona restaurant at Hotel Cedros in Espita, a beautiful town in the heart of the Yucatán. The restaurant sources the finest ingredients, grown just a stone's throw away at Mestiza de Indias, the farm of my friend Gonzalo Samaranch. During my visit to the farm, I made a film documenting the project, and the experience was nothing short of life-changing. It opened my eyes to the true significance of growing our own food – not just for health and wellness, but for the sense of community and empowerment that comes from reclaiming control over our food systems. After spending the day immersed in the farm, tasting that stuffed onion dish felt like a celebration of this humble vegetable, and such was its impact on me that I had to create my own version. The bold flavours of porcini and harissa provide an explosion of taste, perfectly nestled within the delicate, petal-like onion layers.

SERVES 4

3 large onions, peeled

750ml (3 cups) water

For the filling

10g (½ cup/¼oz) dried porcini mushrooms

1 onion, roughly chopped

5 garlic cloves, peeled

100g (1 cup/3½oz) walnuts

Handful of mint leaves

4 tbsp harissa paste

8 sun-dried tomatoes in olive oil

4 tbsp soy sauce or tamari

3 tbsp olive oil

195g (1 cup/7oz) cooked rice

For the roasting liquid

2 tbsp harissa paste

4 tbsp maple syrup

2 tbsp tomato paste

1 tbsp celery salt

1 tbsp garlic granules

4 tbsp olive oil

2 bay leaves

Preheat your oven to 200°C/180°C fan (400°F/Gas Mark 6).

Cut the onions in half vertically, trim the roots a little and peel the layers into individual petals.

Bring the measured water to the boil in a large saucepan, then blanch the onion halves for 5 minutes or until they become pliable. Remove from the water and let them steam dry. Reserve the oniony water and transfer 250ml (1 cup) of it to a bowl or jug (pitcher), keeping the rest for later. Stir in the dried porcini and let them rehydrate for 10 minutes.

Add the rehydrated porcini (keep the soaking liquid) to a food processor along with the chopped onion, garlic, walnuts, mint, harissa, sun-dried tomatoes, soy sauce and olive oil. Blitz until roughly chopped, then transfer to a bowl and stir through the reserved mushroom soaking liquid and the cooked rice.

Cupping an onion petal in the palm of your hand, spoon in 1–2 tablespoons of the filling, then fold the onion over itself and gently squeeze it to seal the filling inside. Place it in a baking dish and repeat with the rest of the onion petals and filling, arranging them in the dish in tight circles.

For the roasting liquid, whisk together 250ml (1 cup) of the reserved onion cooking water with the harissa, maple syrup, tomato paste, celery salt, garlic granules, olive oil and bay leaves.

Pour the roasting liquid over the stuffed onions (pushing the bay leaves in between the onions), then transfer to the oven and roast for 1 hour, or until the liquid has reduced and the onions have caramelized.

'The Bomb' Braised Onion

This dish is called The Bomb, because it packs an explosion of umami. Slowly cooking onions releases a whole new dimension of flavour, especially when cooked with some of the richest ingredients in my pantry. Fermented tofu may be a surprise to you but it can be found in all good Asian stores, or online. It comes in a can and has the most unique, rich flavour. If you can't get your hands on it, just replace it with 2 tablespoons of miso paste.

The recipe is inspired by both mapu tofu and a dish I have whenever I visit NYC: Ivan Ramen's Coney Island-style tofu. This is a rich and powerful, mushroomy, umami plate of food.

SERVES 6

For the braised onion

3 tbsp sesame oil

3 onions, finely chopped

80ml (⅓ cup) rice wine vinegar

3 tbsp Dijon mustard

80ml (⅓ cup) maple syrup

125ml (½ cup) soy sauce

250g (9oz) shiitake mushrooms, finely chopped

½ tsp Szechuan peppercorns, crushed

1 star anise

½ tsp ground cinnamon

2 tbsp minced fresh ginger

6 garlic cloves, minced

2 red chillies, finely sliced

2 tsp miso paste (or 5 tbsp fermented tofu, crumbled – see the introduction)

6 spring onions (scallions), finely chopped

For the tofu

60g (½ cup/2¼oz) cornflour (cornstarch)

2 x 300g (10½oz) blocks of silken tofu, drained

125ml (½ cup) neutral oil, for frying

To garnish

Finely chopped chives

Crispy garlic

Salt and black pepper

Grab a large saucepan and add all the braised onion ingredients except the spring onions. Stir everything really well, then pop a lid on the pan, place over a low heat and leave to braise for about 1 hour, stirring regularly. You want the onions to cook down and the liquids to thicken up until sticky and rich.

Place the cornflour on a plate and season well with salt and pepper. Gently cut the tofu into fillets and dust them in the cornflour. Add the oil to a deep frying pan and, when hot, fry the tofu in batches on all sides until crisp. Remove from the pan and place on a plate lined with kitchen paper to absorb any excess oil.

When the braised onions have cooked down and it's looking like a chunky sauce, it's time to serve up. Stir through the spring onions, arrange your crispy tofu on your plates and spoon over lots of the braised onions. Garnish with chives and crispy garlic.

apple

Apple & Pak Choi Kimchi

Apple is great in kimchi – I actually usually add an apple to most of the kimchis I make, but I thought, why not have a go at making it solely with apples, with some pak choi thrown in for texture... the result is wonderful.

**FILLS A 3-LITRE
(5-PINT) JAR**

5 apples, cored and finely sliced

6 heads of pak choi (bok choy), roughly chopped

3 onions, roughly chopped

10 garlic cloves, finely chopped

Thumb-sized piece of ginger, peeled and finely chopped

2 sheets of dried nori seaweed, torn into small pieces, plus an extra sheet for capping off the kimchi

2 tbsp Korean red chilli flakes (gochugaru)

Sea salt

Place a large bowl on your weighing scales and set the scale to zero, then add all the ingredients except the salt and weigh. Work out what 2% of the weight is, then add that weight in sea salt.

Massage the ingredients together for 5 minutes or so, then cover the bowl with a clean tea (dish) towel. Set aside for at least 2 hours so the natural brine is drawn out.

Transfer the mixture, with the brine, to a sterilized jar(s), then place the sheet of nori directly over the top, plugging the kimchi. Make sure you've added enough brine to cover the mixture by around 1cm (½ inch). Place a glass fermentation weight on top to hold everything beneath the brine (see page 15 for my fermentation troubleshooting guide). The weight is vital, as if any bits end up floating on the surface of the brine during fermentation, yeast/mould will occur and it could spoil.

Cover loosely with the jar lid or a clean tea towel and leave the kimchi to ferment out of the fridge for 7–10 days. Length of fermentation will depend on the temperature of your kitchen. Optimal temperature is around 21°C (70°F). Give the brine a little taste after around the 5-day mark: when it has an acidic tang you like, seal the jar and place it in the fridge, where it can be stored for up to 3 months.

Check the kimchi occasionally to release gas and to look for any signs of yeast on the surface. If you see any, skim it off immediately. The kimchi underneath should still be fine.

Apple, Fennel & Basil Ferment

The perfect blend of sweet and tangy – with a touch of aniseed from the fennel and basil – this is a refreshing ferment you'll love! The bay keeps everything crisp.

FILLS A 3-LITRE (5-PINT) JAR

10 apples, cored

4 fennel bulbs

Sea salt

Small handful of basil leaves

1 bay leaf

Shred the apples and fennel really finely into a large bowl, using either a knife or a mandoline.

Weigh the mixture and add an extra 100g (3½oz) to the figure – to account for extra basil that we will add after. Now work out what 3% of that weight is in sea salt. For example, if the total weight of the ingredients is 300g (10½oz), then 3% would work out as 9g (⅓oz). Add that amount of sea salt to the mixture.

Massage the salt into the apple and fennel really firmly for at least 10 minutes; this will break down the cell walls, helping it release the all-important brine. Stir through the basil and bay leaf.

Cover the bowl with a clean tea (dish) towel and set it aside for 2 hours for all the liquid to be drawn out. After the 2 hours, you should have a lot of liquid. Transfer the mixture, with the brine, to a sterilized jar(s), leaving 2.5cm (1 inch) of headroom at the top of the jar. Make sure you've added enough brine to cover the mixture by around 1cm (½ inch). Place a glass fermentation weight on top to hold everything beneath the brine (see page 15 for my fermentation troubleshooting guide). The weight is vital, as if any bits end up floating on the surface of the brine during fermentation, yeast/mould will occur and it could spoil.

Seal the jars and leave out of the fridge to ferment for up to 14 days. The speed of fermentation depends on the temperature in your kitchen; the warmer it is, the faster it is. Every now and then during fermentation, open the jar to release any gas that may have built up (unless using an airlock where the gas is naturally released).

You can assess the level of fermentation by tasting the brine. The tangier it is, the more fermented it is. Once you've reached your desired level of tang, place the ferment in the fridge. This will slow the fermentation right down and preserve it for months.

Check the ferment occasionally to release gas and to look for any signs of yeast on the surface. If you see any, skim it off immediately. The fruits/veggies underneath should still be fine.

Apple + Pak Choi
Kimchi 4/10

Apple, Sage & Porcini Rolls with Kohlrabi Slaw

MAKES ABOUT 10

15g (1 cup/½oz) dried porcini mushrooms, or 30g (2 cups/1oz) fresh if you're lucky enough to have them

250ml (1 cup) boiling water

3 tbsp olive oil

1 leek, finely sliced

3 garlic cloves, minced

2 apples, cored, peeled and finely chopped

8 sage leaves

2 tsp sea salt

1 tbsp sweet smoked paprika

240g (1½ cups/8oz) canned red kidney beans, rinsed and patted dry

3 tbsp light soy sauce or coconut aminos

1 tsp dried chilli flakes (red pepper flakes)

60g (1 cup/2¼oz) fresh breadcrumbs

5 tbsp plain (all-purpose) flour, plus extra for dusting

1 sheet of ready-rolled puff pastry

For the glaze

2 tbsp oat milk

2 tbsp maple syrup

2 tbsp olive oil

For the apple and kohlrabi slaw

1 green apple, cored

1 kohlrabi

3 tbsp white wine vinegar

3 tbsp maple syrup

¼ tsp caraway seeds

Pinch of sea salt

Apple and porcini is a match made in heaven. Porcini are my favourite mushrooms in the world, and I often forage for them in the Welsh forests near my house. There's nothing quite like their flavour – rich and creamy – and pairing them with apple adds a freshness that cannot be matched.

Add the dried mushrooms to a heatproof bowl and pour over the boiling water. Allow to rehydrate for at least 15 minutes. When plumped up, drain the mushrooms and chop them really finely.

Place a large frying pan over a medium heat and add the oil, leek, garlic, apples, sage and chopped mushrooms. Sauté for 5 minutes, allowing everything to caramelize. Season with the salt as it's cooking. When everything is golden, stir through the smoked paprika, kidney beans, soy sauce, chilli flakes and breadcrumbs. Cook for a few more minutes, then transfer to a large bowl. Add the flour, then use a potato masher to combine the mixture until it begins to hold together. Be careful not to over-mash; you want to retain a chunky texture. Allow the mixture to cool.

Line a baking tray with baking parchment. Whisk the glaze ingredients together in a small bowl. Un-roll the pastry sheet on a lightly floured surface and halve it lengthways with a sharp knife.

Divide the cooled filling between each piece of pastry and shape into log shapes lengthways down the centre of the pastry rectangles. Brush the edges of the pastry with a little of the glaze, then furl the pastry over the filling to seal it completely. Use a fork to firmly press the pastry's edges together, then use a knife to cut the long sausages into 4 or 5 shorter rolls. Place them on the lined baking sheet.

Allow the rolls to chill in the fridge for 20 minutes (or alternatively pop them in the freezer at this stage to enjoy for months to come, cooking directly from frozen). Preheat your oven to 200°C/ 180°C fan (400°F/Gas Mark 6).

Brush the tops and sides of the rolls with the remaining glaze, prick them with a fork and bake for 35 minutes, until golden brown.

Meanwhile, using a mandoline, finely slice the apple and kohlrabi. Add them to a bowl with the rest of the slaw ingredients, mix well and leave to marinate for 5 or so minutes.

Serve the apple and porcini rolls with the slaw, and some homemade brown sauce (see page 216).

Chunky Apple & Ginger Spelt Pie, with Chamomile Custard

Chamomile and apple is a surprising flavour combination that just works, and both are grown in my garden. Everyone should have a pot of chamomile flowers growing somewhere, as it's great as a calming tea or infused into dishes like this. I use spelt flour, an ancient grain native to the UK that has a nutty flavour. All-purpose wheat flour is so mass produced these days that choosing a flour like spelt or another ancient grain flour will not only be better for you and the planet, but will add a uniqueness to your dishes.

SERVES 8

8 cooking apples, such as Bramley

130g (¾ cup/4½oz) coconut sugar

1 tbsp vanilla extract

4 tbsp crystallized ginger, finely chopped

Zest and juice of 1 lemon

¼ tsp ground cinnamon

2 tbsp cornflour (cornstarch)

Chamomile flowers, to decorate

For the pastry

280g (2 cups/10oz) spelt flour, plus extra for dusting

½ tsp sea salt

1 tbsp caster (superfine) sugar, plus extra for sprinkling on top

150g (⅔ cup/5½oz) cold butter, cubed, plus extra for greasing

4 tbsp ice-cold water

Peel and core the apples, then cut them into 3cm (1¼ inch) cubes (save the peel to make tea, see page 213).

Add three-quarters of the apples to a medium saucepan, along with the coconut sugar, vanilla, ginger, lemon zest and juice and cinnamon, then place over a medium heat. Cook until the apple begins to break down, around 15 minutes. Give it a light mash with a fork, then stir through the reserved apple cubes.

In a small bowl, mix the cornflour with a little water until smooth, then stir it into the apple mixture. Continue to cook until the filling thickens and turns jammy, then remove from the heat and allow to cool completely.

Next, make the pastry. In a large bowl, mix together the flour, salt and caster sugar. Add the cold, cubed butter and use your fingers to work the butter into the flour mixture until it resembles breadcrumbs. Gradually add the cold water, a little at a time, mixing just until the dough comes together, then knead the dough for a couple of minutes before wrapping it and allowing to rest in the fridge for at least 15 minutes.

Grease a 23cm (9-inch) pie dish that is quite deep. Place a large sheet of baking parchment on your work surface and flour it generously; this will help you easily lift the pastry into your dish. Roll out three-quarters of the pastry on your floured sheet until it's slightly larger than your pie dish (don't go thinner than about 3mm/⅛ inch). Pick up the sheet and invert it into your pie dish, then peel off the baking parchment.

Continued...

For the glaze

3 tbsp maple syrup

3 tbsp olive oil

2 tbsp oat milk

For the chamomile custard

1 x 400g (14oz) can of coconut milk

2 chamomile tea bags

¼ tsp ground turmeric

4 tbsp maple syrup

3 tbsp cornflour (cornstarch)

Gently press the pastry into all the corners of the pie dish and up the sides, trim off any excess pastry, then prick the base with a fork. Place the pastry base in the freezer for at least 20 minutes; this will stop the pastry shrinking when it bakes.

Preheat your oven to 200°C/180°C fan (400°F/Gas Mark 6). Whip up the glaze ingredients in a small bowl.

After its time in the freezer, it's time to blind bake the pastry to achieve a crispy base. Place a sheet of baking parchment in the centre of the pie dish and fill with a cup or so of baking beans or uncooked rice – you just need something to hold down the pastry while it's cooking. Bake for 15 minutes on the bottom shelf of your oven, then remove the beans and paper and bake for a further 5 minutes.

Meanwhile, roll out the remaining pastry for the top of the pie.

Fill the blind-baked pastry case with your apple mixture, then cover with the pastry top. Crimp the edges with a fork to seal the top to the pie dish, then trim any excess pastry. You can get creative with the topping pastry, with lattice or fancy shapes if you like. Just make sure you cut a few slits or pierce it with a fork to allow the steam to escape. Brush the pie with the remaining glaze and sprinkle over a little sugar. Bake for 45–50 minutes until the crust is golden and the filling is bubbling.

To make the custard, pour the coconut milk into a small saucepan with the chamomile tea bags. Bring to a simmer for 5 minutes, then stir in the turmeric and maple syrup. In a small bowl, whisk the cornflour with a little water to create a smooth paste. Remove the tea bags, then whisk the cornflour mix into the coconut milk. Turn the heat to low and let the custard thicken up slightly.

When the pie is cooked, cut a big slice and serve with a dollop of custard. I like to garnish it with a few fresh chamomile flowers too, if I have them.

Calming Apple Peel Tea

Making an infusion blend with apple peels is a great way to use them up; there's a lot of aroma, flavour and healing benefits in the peel which we can utilize in a herbal infusion. Calming ingredients like lavender, chamomile, lemon balm and rose petals contribute to the tea's soothing and calming effect, making it an ideal drink for relaxation. Simply scale the quantities up or down depending on how many apples you want to use.

**MAKES AS MUCH OR
AS LITTLE AS YOU LIKE**

Peel from at least 6 apples

Dried lavender

Dried chamomile flowers

Dried lemon balm leaves

Dried rose petals

Preheat your oven to its lowest temperature and line a baking tray with baking parchment. Spread the apple peels evenly on the tray and place in the oven to dry for 2–3 hours, until fully dried and crispy. Remove from the oven and let cool completely. This part can also be done in a dehydrator if you have one.

To two parts apple, add one part each of lavender, chamomile, lemon balm and rose petals. So if you have 1 cup of dried apple peel, you'd add half a cup of each of the other ingredients. Mix everything up in a bowl and store in a sealed jar.

To brew the tea, add about 2 tablespoons of the mixture to a tea infuser or tea pot. Pour boiling water over and let it steep for 5–7 minutes. Strain into a cup and enjoy, ideally 2 hours before bedtime. The dried mixture will store well for months in a cool, dark place.

Classic British Brown Sauce

When researching old British condiment recipes, it struck me that apple is always used as a sweetener in classic brown sauce. I guess its natural sugars plus tartness are a valued note in the delicious sauce. It's another way to use up and preserve the abundant apple harvests.

MAKES 1 LITRE (2 PINTS)

4 Bramley apples, peeled, cored and cubed

2 large onions, roughly chopped

8 garlic cloves, peeled

2 tbsp chopped fresh ginger

2 tbsp olive oil

12 dates, pitted and very finely chopped

300g (3 cups/10½oz) raisins, very finely chopped

3 tsp ground allspice

3 tsp mustard powder

3 tsp sea salt

3 bay leaves

2 cinnamon sticks

2 tsp ground black pepper

500ml (2 cups) malt vinegar

500ml (2 cups) apple juice

120ml (½ cup) maple syrup

200g (1 cup/7oz) dark brown sugar

5 tbsp tomato paste

60ml (¼ cup) light soy sauce

Add the apples, onions, garlic and ginger to a food processor and blitz until super fine.

Place a medium saucepan over a low heat and add the oil. When hot, add the blitzed apple mixture and sauté for 5 minutes until well sweated down and slightly caramelized.

Stir through the chopped dates and raisins and cook for a few more minutes before adding the allspice, mustard powder, salt, bay leaves, cinnamon and pepper.

Deglaze the pan with the vinegar, apple juice and maple syrup. Stir well and let the mix bubble away for 5 minutes. Add the sugar, tomato paste and soy sauce and leave to cook away slowly for about an hour; you're wanting to achieve a sticky, saucy consistency. Stir often to avoid the bottom from catching.

When the sauce is sticky, transfer it to a blender and blitz until super smooth. Let cool, then pour it into sterilized glass jars or bottles and seal tightly. Store the jars in the fridge, where it will last for up to 3 months.

Kale & Apple Salad, with Maple & Peanut

A fresh and vibrant salad with a punch; the apple cuts through the richness of the peanuts perfectly. I grow Thai basil in my greenhouse and it adds a unique aniseed-like flavour, but it can also be bought at most supermarkets. I choose a sweet, crisp apple, like a Braeburn, for this – the red skin also looks great among the green leaves. Massaging kale is so underrated; once you've had it like this you won't go back!

SERVES 2-4

70g (½ cup/2½oz) raw shelled peanuts

1 tbsp peanut oil

4 tbsp maple syrup

1 tbsp smooth peanut butter

2 tsp miso paste

4 tbsp sauerkraut or kimchi brine, or rice wine vinegar

4 spring onions (scallions), finely chopped

1 red chilli, finely chopped

1 garlic clove, minced

Pinch of sea salt

200g (7oz) curly kale

2 apples (I use red Braeburns), cored and finely sliced

Handful of Thai basil, or an aromatic herb like coriander (cilantro)

Preheat your oven to 200°C/180°C fan (400°F/Gas Mark 6).

Place the peanuts onto a small roasting tray and roast in the oven for 8–9 minutes, keeping an eye on them as they can burn quickly.

In a large bowl, whisk together the peanut oil, maple syrup, peanut butter, miso, brine, spring onions, chilli, garlic and salt.

Tear the kale into the bowl, discarding the stems (compost them). Wash your hands thoroughly, then massage the dressing firmly into the kale for about 2 minutes. Be rough; this will break down the cell walls in the kale, making it easily digestible.

Stir the apple through the kale along with the roasted peanuts and Thai basil, then serve up right away.

Roasted Celeriac, Apple & Fennel Soup, with Crispy Garlic

This is a simple soup using some of my all-time favourite ingredients, and roasting everything together adds a new dimension of flavour. Don't discard the apple peel – see page 213 for a tea I make using the peels. This soup is super creamy and garnished with crispy garlic.

SERVES 4

1 celeriac (celery root), peeled and cubed

5 apples, cored, peeled and cubed

3 fennel bulbs, roughly chopped

2 onions, roughly chopped

4 garlic cloves, peeled

5 tbsp olive oil

3 tbsp maple syrup

1 tsp fennel seeds

2 tsp sea salt

½ tsp cracked black pepper

1.5 litres (6 cups) good-quality vegetable stock

125ml (½ cup) cashew nut milk, or any creamy milk you like

Juice of ½ lemon

Garden herbs (like fennel fronds, carrot tops, sage, marjoram, thyme), to serve (optional)

For the crispy garlic

60ml (¼ cup) olive oil

6–8 garlic cloves, sliced super thin

Pinch of sea salt

Preheat your oven to 200°C/180°C fan (400°F/Gas Mark 6).

Bundle the celeriac, apples, fennel, onions and garlic onto a roasting tray then drizzle over the olive oil and maple syrup. Season with the fennel seeds, salt and pepper. Toss everything together, then roast in the oven for around 45 minutes, or until golden and soft.

Carefully add everything to a blender, along with the stock (do this in batches if you need to), then blitz until super smooth and it has a soupy consistency. If your blender isn't that powerful, you can always pass the soup through a sieve (strainer), for a smoother texture.

Transfer the soup to a saucepan and stir through the milk. Check if it's seasoned nicely, then add the lemon juice to bring the soup to life. Keep warm.

For the crispy garlic, pour the oil into a small pan over a medium to low heat. Once the oil is hot, add the sliced garlic to the pan. Stir occasionally to make sure it's cooking evenly and to stop it burning. Fry until the garlic turns a light golden brown, about 1–2 minutes. Be careful, as garlic can burn quickly. Using a slotted spoon, remove the crispy garlic slices from the oil and place on a plate lined with kitchen paper to soak up any excess oil. Season with a pinch of salt to keep them crisp.

Serve the soup with lots of crispy garlic and a few garden herbs (if you have them) scattered on top.

Stuffed Campfire Apples

These are perfect for the autumn months, when there is nothing I love more than getting wrapped up and spending the day outside in the crisp air. Both the cooking and eating of these makes me feel so nostalgic – they're a perfect Bonfire Night snack.

SERVES 8

300g (2 cups/10½oz) mixed nuts

100g (1 cup/3½oz) dried cherries, roughly chopped

85g (½ cup/3oz) coconut sugar

3 tbsp fresh lemon thyme leaves, plus extra to serve

1 tbsp ground cinnamon

4 tbsp maple syrup, plus extra to serve

½ tsp sea salt

8 apples

To serve

Ice cream (see page 140 for homemade)

Start a fire in your fire pit, and leave to blaze down to hot coals. Place a large Dutch oven pan over your fire or on your BBQ to preheat.

Blitz the nuts and add them to a mixing bowl with the cherries, coconut sugar, thyme leaves, cinnamon, maple syrup and salt. Mix really well, then set aside.

Cut the tops off the apples, then core each one, removing the seeds and a little flesh to create a cavity for the filling (compost the cores), then stuff each cavity with the nut and cherry mixture.

Place the tops back on each apple, then stand them right-way up into your Dutch oven and cover with the lid. Carefully gather hot coals and place them on top of the lid. Push coals all around the sides of the pot, making sure there's an even amount of heat all around.

Let the apples bake for around 1 hour, until cooked, slightly golden and smelling delicious. Serve them up with a little ice cream and top with some extra maple syrup and fresh thyme leaves.

Whole Roasted Apple Bara Brith

This is my all-time favourite dessert. I don't eat a lot of sugar, but this is an exception. I've put a spin on this childhood classic by baking whole apples and placing them in the centre of the cake. Bara brith translates from Welsh as 'speckled bread'.

MAKES 2 LOAVES (SERVES ABOUT 12)

300g (1½ cups/10½oz) mixed dried fruit, such as sultanas (golden raisins), currants, raisins and candied mixed peel

3 tbsp chia seeds

500ml (2 cups) strong freshly brewed black tea

4 apples (something like Cox is ideal), peeled but leave the stalks and cores intact

5 tbsp caster (superfine) sugar

½ tsp ground cinnamon

220g (1¼ cups/7¾oz) brown sugar

80ml (⅓ cup) olive oil, plus a little extra for greasing

400g (2¾ cups/14oz) self-raising flour

½ tsp fine sea salt

1 tbsp ground mixed spice

Start by chopping the dried fruit quite finely before placing it in a large bowl with the chia seeds. Pour over the hot tea, then allow the fruit to soak it up and slightly plump up for around 2 hours.

Preheat your oven to 200°C/180°C fan (400°F/Gas Mark 6). Grease two 450g (1lb) loaf tins (pans) with a little olive oil and line them with baking parchment.

Place the apples in a roasting tray, sprinkle over the caster sugar and cinnamon, then roast in the oven for 25 minutes.

Once the dried fruit has plumped up, fold the brown sugar and olive oil through the mixture until well incorporated. Then sift the flour, salt and mixed spice into the bowl and mix lightly until just combined – don't over-mix.

Spoon around a 4cm (1½-inch) depth of cake mixture into the base of each loaf tin, then place 2 roasted apples into each, stalk-side up. Spoon the remaining cake batter all around the apples, filling the loaf tins.

Bake in the oven for 30 minutes, then cover the tins with foil and bake for a further 25 minutes. Remove from the oven but leave covered for another 20 minutes to finish cooking through.

When cooled, slice thickly and enjoy. You can also toast the slices in a non-stick pan to make them deliciously crisp.

pumpkin
& squash

Fermented Pumpkin Seed Log

Believe it or not, this is very similar to a cheese. In fact, it has all the attributes to be called a cheese: it's creamy and tangy thanks to the pumpkin seeds and the power of fermentation.

SERVES 12

130g (1 cup/4½oz) pumpkin seeds, soaked in water for at least 2 hours

130g (1 cup/4½oz) macadamia nuts, soaked in water for at least 2 hours

240ml (1 cup) filtered water

5 tbsp nutritional yeast

1 tsp garlic granules

1 tsp smoked paprika

Juice of ½ lemon

1 tbsp white miso paste

½ teaspoon sea salt

2 probiotic capsules, such as acidophilus

For the coating

3 tbsp cracked black pepper

1 tbsp finely chopped rosemary

Start by draining the soaked pumpkin seeds and macadamia nuts. It's important they've been soaked for at least 2 hours to soften properly. Then, in a high-speed blender, combine the drained seeds and nuts with the filtered water, nutritional yeast, garlic, paprika, lemon juice, miso, salt and probiotic capsules.

Blend until super smooth, scraping the sides of the blender every now and then with a spatula to ensure there are no lumps.

When super smooth, transfer the mixture to a nut milk bag or sheet of cheesecloth. In a warm, dry place where it won't be disturbed, use string and a wooden spoon to suspend the mixture in a large bowl so any liquid can slowly drip out. Cover the bowl with cling film (plastic wrap) and leave to ferment for 48 hours. The fermentation time can vary depending on the room temperature and how tangy you'd like it; the ideal temperature is 23°C (73°F).

Taste the mixture – it should be tangy and very savoury. If it's to your liking, you can use it immediately as a cream cheese-style spread, or for a firmer texture, place it in the fridge. It will continue to firm up and develop flavour over the next few days.

When it's firm enough to roll, roll the mixture into a log shape. Combine the black pepper and rosemary on a plate, then roll the log in it to coat.

Wrap the log in baking parchment and store in the fridge for up to 1 month.

Pumpkin & Pearl Barley Stew with Nettle Dressing

This is a super-hearty and wholesome stew, finished off with a taste of vibrant nettle, which I always have an abundance of in my garden (best picked with gloves when the plants are young). Pearl barley is very underrated and a great source of many vitamins and minerals that our bodies need. Roasting the pumpkin separately adds a deep caramelization, resulting in a much better flavour than if you were to just throw the pumpkin in raw.

SERVES 4, GENEROUSLY

5 tbsp olive oil

1 onion, finely chopped

3 garlic cloves, minced

2 celery sticks, very finely chopped

1 sprig of rosemary

5 sage leaves, finely chopped

400g (2 cups/14oz) pearl barley, thoroughly rinsed

250ml (1 cup) white wine

1 litre (4 cups) vegetable stock

360g (13oz) pumpkin, sliced

1 red onion, chopped into chunks

2 tsp cracked black pepper

Sea salt

For the nettle (or spinach) dressing

100g (3½oz) young nettle leaves (or use baby spinach)

4 spring onions (scallions)

1 garlic clove, peeled

4 tbsp ferment brine, or lemon juice

125ml (½ cup) extra virgin olive oil

To garnish

Dried chilli (red pepper) flakes

Pumpkin seeds

Preheat your oven to 220°C/200°C fan (425°F/Gas Mark 7).

Place a large saucepan over a medium heat and add 1 tablespoon of the olive oil, followed by the onion, garlic, celery, rosemary and sage, then sauté for about 5 minutes, until softened.

Stir in the pearl barley and let it toast slightly in the pan for a couple of minutes before deglazing with the wine. Bring to a simmer, then add the stock, stirring well. Let the stock come to a simmer, pop a lid on the pan and allow the pearl barley to cook away for 30 minutes, stirring every now and then.

Meanwhile, grab a roasting tray and toss the pumpkin and red onion chunks in the remaining 4 tablespoons of olive oil, along with the cracked black pepper and 1 teaspoon of salt. Spread them out evenly on the tray and roast until the pumpkin is cooked through and caramelized.

For the nettle dressing, blanch the nettles (or spinach) in boiling water for 30–45 seconds, then drain and rinse under cold water. Pat and squeeze any excess liquid of out the nettles, using a clean tea (dish) towel, then transfer them to a blender with the spring onions, garlic, brine or lemon juice, olive oil and salt to taste. Blend until saucy but still a little chunky.

Check the pearl barley is tender by tasting one or two grains, then stir the pumpkin and red onion through the stew and season if you feel it needs it. Serve garnished with the nettle dressing, some chilli flakes and, of course, some mighty pumpkin seeds.

Pumpkin Croquettes

These are somewhere between pumpkin katsu and pumpkin croquettes. I add a little spice to the pumpkin filling with one of my favourite spice blends of all time: Chinese five spice. Serve them with my fermented hot sauce (page 182) or carrot ribbon and chard kimchi (page 71).

MAKES 10-12

1 small pumpkin, about 500g (1lb 2oz)

1 tbsp onion granules

1 tbsp garlic granules

½ tsp Chinese five spice

4 tbsp plain (all-purpose) flour, plus extra for dusting

3 tbsp olive oil

2 tsp sea salt

1 tsp dried chilli flakes (red pepper flakes)

3 spring onions (scallions), chopped

3 tbsp soy sauce

125ml (½ cup) neutral oil, for frying

Hot sauce and/or carrot kimchi emulsion (see pages 182 and 81), to serve

For the coating

50g (1¾oz) panko breadcrumbs (or gluten-free alternative)

3 tbsp sesame seeds

280g (2 cups/10oz) plain (all-purpose) flour (or gluten-free alternative)

First, prepare your pumpkin. Peel (using a serrated knife – it's always easier), deseed, then chop it into small cubes. Steam the cubes until tender (I recommend steaming here, but you can always boil or even roast them; you just want mashable pumpkin), then mash until smooth.

Put the mashed pumpkin in a large bowl with the onion and garlic granules, Chinese five spice, flour, olive oil, salt, chilli flakes, spring onions and soy sauce, and mix together until really well combined. If it's not coming together (it should be mouldable), then add a little more flour.

Grab a tray and dust it with a little flour. Leave some on your hands, too. Next, take tablespoons of the pumpkin mixture and shape each into a cylinder or round, lightly dusting them with more flour after putting them on the tray. You should have about 10–12. Pop the tray in the freezer while you prepare the coating.

Grab 3 small, shallow bowls and in one mix the panko breadcrumbs with the sesame seeds. Place half the coating flour in another, and in the final bowl whisk together the remaining flour with enough water to create a pancake batter-style consistency.

Dip each croquette first in the flour, then the batter, and finally in the panko and sesame seed mixture, making sure the croquettes are coated all over. Try to keep one hand for dry and one for wet (or you'll breadcrumb your fingers).

Heat the oil in a heavy-based skillet or large saucepan (ensuring the oil comes no further than halfway up the sides of the pan) set over a medium heat. Bring it to about 180°C (356°F). To test if the oil is hot enough, place a wooden spoon in the pan; if bubbles form around the spoon, it is hot enough to fry. Fry the croquettes in batches, until golden and crispy on all sides. Once fried, transfer to a plate lined with kitchen paper to absorb any excess oil.

Serve the croquettes hot, with some hot sauce or carrot kimchi emulsion on the side.

Pumpkin Seed & Apricot Energy Bars

I feel we should be eating way more pumpkin seeds – they're so good for us. They are packed with zinc, which is particularly great for men's health, and also with healthy fats and magnesium, which are great for the heart. The mix of chia and hemp seeds adds a nice punch of protein and omega-3s, while the oats provide slow-burning energy to keep you going. I tend to eat one of these pre-workout, or cut them small, wrap them up and take them on long runs or cycles.

MAKES 8-10

300g (10½oz) pitted dates

130g (1 cup/4½oz) dried apricots, plus extra for topping

130g (1 cup/4½oz) pumpkin seeds, plus extra for topping

65g (½ cup/2½oz) roasted nuts, such as pistachio or hazelnut (optional)

60g (½ cup/2oz) hemp seeds

35g (¼ cup/1¼oz) chia seeds

90g (1 cup/3¼oz) oats

Pinch of sea salt

½ tsp ground cinnamon

100g (3½oz) dark (bittersweet) chocolate, melted

Add the dates and apricots to a food processor and blend until they form a sticky paste.

Add the remaining ingredients (except the melted chocolate) to a large bowl and mix really well.

Add the date and apricot paste to the dry ingredients and then use a spoon or your hands to mix everything together until fully combined.

Line a baking dish, about 20 x 25cm (8 x 10 inches), with baking parchment. Transfer the mixture to the dish and press it down firmly into an even layer, using a spatula or the back of a spoon. Top the mixture with a few extra pumpkin seeds and apricots, then drizzle all over with the melted chocolate. Place in the fridge to set for at least 30 minutes.

Once firm, remove the block from the dish and cut it into bars or shapes of your choice. The energy bars can be stored in an airtight container in the fridge for a few weeks.

Roasted Pumpkin Ravioli

I have a special connection to making my own pasta. I taught myself as a young kid how to roll homemade pasta and then, when I entered professional kitchens and had to make hundreds of ravioli, it was a chance to focus and have a moment of calm amid the chaos. The vibrant pumpkin filling bursts out when you cut into these ravioli and melts into the creamy sauce so beautifully. Making a dish like this is everything I love about the art of cooking – it's pure therapy.

SERVES 4

For the filling

1 small pumpkin, deseeded (unpeeled) and cut into chunks

1 onion, peeled and halved

1 whole garlic bulb, halved horizontally

2 tsp dried chilli flakes (red pepper flakes)

8 sage leaves

4 tbsp olive oil

4 tbsp balsamic vinegar

4 tbsp maple syrup

Pinch each of sea salt and cracked black pepper

50g (½ cup/1¾oz) walnuts or pine nuts, toasted

For the pasta

260g (2 cups/9oz) 00 pasta flour, plus extra for dusting

½ tsp salt

¼ tsp ground turmeric

160ml (⅔ cup) water

2 tbsp olive oil

Preheat your oven to 200°C/180°C fan (400°F/Gas Mark 6).

Place the pumpkin on a roasting tray with the onion halves, garlic bulb halves, chilli flakes, sage, olive oil, vinegar, maple syrup, salt and pepper. Use your hands to toss the ingredients together, making sure everything is nicely coated. Roast in the oven for about 40 minutes, until tender and caramelized.

Meanwhile, in a bowl, mix the pasta ingredients together until it comes together into a ball of dough. Knead for around 8 minutes until smooth and elasticated, then let the dough rest in the fridge for about 30 minutes.

Remove the pumpkin tray from the oven, then squeeze the garlic cloves from their skins and add them to a blender with the rest of the roasted ingredients. (I often leave the skins on the pumpkin, but if you prefer, they can be removed.) Add the toasted walnuts or pine nuts and pulse until just puréed; a few lumps won't hurt. The filling needs to be quite thick, so if it's on the wet side, add a few tablespoons of flour.

Allow the filling to cool completely, then dust your work surface with a little flour, ready to roll out your pasta dough to a thin sheet, using a pasta machine or rolling pin.

I roll mine to the second-to-last thinness on the machine, then use a pastry cutter to cut circles. I cut two different sizes, one around 5cm (2 inches) and one 6cm (2½ inches). The smaller disc will be for the base, and the larger for the top (it needs to be big enough to hang over the lump of filling in the centre of the base and then meet up with the edge of the base).

For the sauce

3 tbsp olive oil, plus extra to serve

6–8 sage leaves, finely chopped

3 garlic cloves, minced

1 small shallot, finely chopped

60ml (¼ cup) white wine or vegetable stock

250ml (1 cup) cream (I use oat)

30g (½ cup/1oz) nutritional yeast

2 tsp miso paste

Pinch each of sea salt and cracked black pepper

Pinch of ground nutmeg

Squeeze of lemon juice

1 tbsp finely chopped chives

Toasted pumpkin seeds, to serve

Place a small amount of the filling in the centre of each smaller pasta disc, ensuring you don't overfill them. Moisten the edges of the dough with a little water and place a large circle on top. Seal the edges firmly by pressing down with your fingers. Make sure the ravioli are well sealed to prevent the filling from escaping during cooking. Continue the process until you've used up all your pasta and filling. If you have leftover filling, it can be frozen and used for future dishes. The ravioli can also be frozen at this stage and then enjoyed at your leisure, cooked from frozen.

If cooking them right away, I recommend popping them in the fridge to firm up slightly before cooking.

Before serving, make the sauce. Heat the olive oil in a medium frying pan over a medium heat. Add the sage, garlic and shallot and cook until the onion is caramelized and the sage is a little crisp. Pour in the wine or stock and allow to cook away and reduce slightly for 4–5 minutes, then stir in the cream, nutritional yeast, miso, salt, pepper and nutmeg, letting the sauce simmer away and thicken up. Finish it with a squeeze of lemon juice and the chives.

To cook the ravioli, bring a large saucepan of salted water to the boil, add the ravioli and poach for 2–3 minutes or until they float to the surface. Drain, gently toss them in the sauce and serve up right away, garnished with a little olive oil and toasted pumpkin seeds.

Sikil Pak with Panisse
& Roasted Pumpkin

Sikil pak is a pumpkin seed dish from the Yucatán peninsula of Mexico and is cherished by the Mayan people, who have cultivated squash and pumpkins forever. I discovered sikil pak on a life-changing trip to Mexico a few years back. The gracious welcome I had from the Mayan people in Yucatán was something I will never forget, and tasting authentic sikil pak was the experience of a lifetime. Since that trip, whenever I harvest one of my pumpkins, the piles of seeds found inside are celebrated as much as the pumpkin flesh; I dry them so that I have a supply to make my sikil pak for months to come (although you can use store-bought). I wanted to serve this with something different – with crunch – and I looked to France and Italy for inspiration: a panisse is a decadent, unbelievably moreish fried chickpea slice. The two go so well together.

SERVES 6

For the sikil pak

130g (1 cup/4½oz) pumpkin seeds

2 tomatoes

5 spring onions (scallions), trimmed

1 jalapeño chilli

3 garlic cloves, peeled

½ tsp ground cumin

Handful of coriander (cilantro)

½ tsp sea salt

Juice of 1 lime

For the panisse

1 litre (4 cups) vegetable stock

280g (2 cup/10oz) chickpea (gram) flour

2 tsp garlic granules

Juice of 1 lemon

4 tbsp olive oil, plus extra for frying and greasing

1 tsp fine sea salt

To serve

Roasted pumpkin cubes

Preheat your oven to 200°C/180°C fan (400°F/Gas Mark 6).

Grab two baking trays, and on one of them spread out the pumpkin seeds. On the other, place the tomatoes, spring onions, jalapeño and garlic. Place both trays in the oven (pumpkin seeds on the very bottom of the oven, right beneath the tomato tray) and roast for 15–20 minutes, until the pumpkin seeds are nicely toasted.

Allow the pumpkin seeds to cool slightly, then transfer them to a blender and blitz to a fine crumb. Add the roasted tomatoes, spring onions, chilli and garlic, along with the remaining sikil pak ingredients, and pulse until the mixture comes together and looks like a chunky dip. This will store for up to a week in the fridge.

To make the panisse, bring the stock to a simmer in a large saucepan and lightly grease a 20 x 20cm (8 x 8-inch) baking tin.

When the stock is simmering, reduce the heat to low and whisk in the chickpea flour. Continue to whisk for 6–8 minutes until it resembles polenta. Take off the heat and whisk in the garlic granules, lemon juice, olive oil and salt until thick and completely smooth. Pour the batter into the greased baking tin and spread it evenly using a spatula. Allow it to cool at room temperature, then cover and refrigerate for at least 1 hour, or until fully set.

Once set, turn the panisse out onto a board and cut it into large chips/sticks. Heat enough olive oil for shallow frying in a cast-iron pan over a medium heat, and fry the panisse in batches for 3–4 minutes on each side, until golden and crisp on all sides. Transfer to a plate lined with kitchen paper, to drain excess oil.

Serve the panisse with plenty of your pumpkin seed sikil pak, and a few chunks of roasted pumpkin.

Cinnamon Spiced
Sourdough Doughnuts

Making these sweet doughnuts with my sourdough starter and homegrown pumpkin makes me feel very self-sufficient. I grow some big pumpkins, which means I'm always looking for creative ways to use them up – this particular experiment was an instant winner, and the perfect autumn treat.

Make sure you start this recipe the day before you want to enjoy the doughnuts, to give the sourdough a chance to work its magic.

Please be extra careful when frying, as the oil is extremely hot and can be dangerous. Make sure your pan is at the back of your stove and never drop the doughnuts in.

MAKES 10-12

200g (¾ cup/7oz) refreshed (very bubbly!) sourdough starter (see *Note* overleaf)

240g (1 cup/8oz) mashed pumpkin or pumpkin purée

250ml (1 cup) almond milk

3 tbsp olive oil

3 tbsp maple syrup

525g (3¾ cups/18½oz) strong white bread flour, plus extra for dusting

2 tsp ground cinnamon

½ tsp ground nutmeg

½ tsp ground allspice

2 tsp ground ginger

1 tsp sea salt

1 litre (4 cups) neutral oil, for frying

For the coating

100g (½ cup/3½oz) date or coconut sugar

2 tsp ground cinnamon

¼ tsp ground nutmeg

The night before you want to eat your doughnuts, in a large bowl mix together the sourdough starter, pumpkin, almond milk, olive oil and maple syrup until everything is well combined.

In a separate bowl, mix together the flour, spices and salt. Gently fold the dry ingredients into the wet sourdough mixture, stirring until it forms a dough.

Dust your work surface with a little flour, then transfer the dough onto it and knead for about 8–10 minutes, until smooth and elastic. If the dough is sticky, you can add a little more flour, but avoid adding too much.

Lightly oil a clean, large bowl, then place the dough in it and cover it with a damp cloth. Place somewhere warm to rise and double in size overnight. This should take around 12 hours, but longer in colder temperatures.

The next morning, dust your work surface with a little flour and turn the dough out. Roll it into a large rectangle around 1.25cm (½ inch) thick, then use pastry cutters to cut the dough into doughnut shapes of your choice – I use a 10cm (4-inch) and 2.5cm (1-inch) cutter to create ring doughnuts and mini doughnut balls respectively.

Carefully place the doughnuts on a flat tray lined with baking parchment dusted with flour, and cover it over with a damp tea (dish) towel or cling film (plastic wrap). Leave to rise somewhere warm for at least 45 minutes.

Continued...

Meanwhile, toss together the coating ingredients in a bowl big enough to dip your doughnuts in once they're cooked.

When your doughnuts have risen and are ready to fry, heat the oil in a heavy-based skillet or large saucepan (ensuring the oil comes no further than halfway up the sides of the pan) set over a medium heat. Bring it to about 180°C (356°F). To test if the oil is hot enough, place a wooden spoon in the pan; if bubbles form around the spoon, it is hot enough to fry.

Gently pick up the risen doughnuts and carefully lower them into the oil, cooking one or two at a time. Fry for around 3–4 minutes (or half the time for the mini doughnut balls) until golden, gently turning them over halfway through cooking. Keep an eye on the temperature of your oil; if your doughnuts colour too fast, turn the heat down.

Use a slotted spoon or spider to lift the cooked doughnuts out of the oil, then onto a tray lined with kitchen paper to drain excess oil.

While still hot, toss the doughnuts in your spice sugar mix, then serve straight away.

Note
Instead of deep frying, you can bake the doughnuts in an oven preheated to 220°C/200°C fan (425°F/Gas Mark 7) for 30 minutes.

If you don't have a sourdough starter you can replace it with 7g (2 tsp) fast action dried yeast and simply begin on the day you want to bake the doughnuts (instead of the day before). If doing so, you'll also need to increase the almond milk to 310ml (1¼ cups) and the strong white bread flour to 625g (4½ cups). Gently warm the almond milk until tepid, then add the yeast and let it sit for 5–10 minutes until frothy. Combine the yeast-milk mixture with the pumpkin, olive oil and maple syrup then proceed with the recipe as directed, proving the dough for 1–2 hours until doubled in size (instead of 12 hours).

Whipped Pumpkin Polenta with Braised Kale & Mushrooms

This dish is simply me on a plate. If it could have been the front page of this book, then I would have chosen it. It is cosy and humble but fancy at the same time. It sings of autumn, and I'll often make it with mushrooms I've foraged from the woodlands around me during the season.

SERVES 4

1 small pumpkin, deseeded (unpeeled) and cut into wedges

6 tbsp olive oil, plus extra for roasting the pumpkin and frying the mushrooms

1 whole garlic bulb

500ml (2 cups) vegetable stock

250ml (1 cup) milk

150g (1 cup/5½oz) quick-cook polenta (cornmeal)

3 tbsp maple syrup

Pinch of ground nutmeg

450g (16oz) wild mushrooms, such as chanterelles or king oysters, halved or quartered if large

Sea salt

For the braised kale

3 tbsp olive oil

1 small shallot, finely sliced

3 garlic cloves, finely sliced

6 cavolo nero stems, leaves torn into strips

3 sprigs of thyme

125ml (½ cup) white wine

To garnish

Fresh thyme leaves

Toasted hazelnuts

Preheat your oven to 220°C/200°C fan (425°F/Gas Mark 7).

Place the pumpkin wedges on a baking tray, drizzle with olive oil and season with a pinch of salt. Add the whole garlic bulb to the tray and roast for about 25–30 minutes, or until the pumpkin is tender and slightly caramelized. Once cool enough to handle, remove the pumpkin flesh from the skin and mash it with a fork. Cut the garlic bulb in half horizontally, squeeze the cloves out into the pumpkin and mash, mixing them together.

Add the stock and milk to a large saucepan and bring to a simmer. Slowly whisk in the polenta, then switch to a spatula and constantly stir to avoid any lumps. Turn the heat down to low and cook the polenta, stirring often until it thickens and becomes creamy. Stir through the mashed pumpkin, the 6 tablespoons of olive oil, the maple syrup and nutmeg, whipping the mixture with a whisk until it becomes silky. Add a touch more liquid if you feel it needs it.

Set a large pan over a medium-high heat and add the mushrooms. As they cook, they will release liquid – once this has almost evaporated, add a drizzle of olive oil and some salt and pepper and fry for a couple of minutes until the mushrooms are golden. Transfer to a warm plate and set the pan back over a medium heat.

Add the olive oil for the kale to the pan, then add the sliced shallot and garlic and cook until a little golden. Add the cavolo nero and thyme and cook for a minute before deglazing with the wine. Season with a pinch of salt, then cover the pan and let the kale braise for 2–3 minutes, stirring now and then.

To serve, spoon the whipped pumpkin polenta onto your plates and top with the braised kale and sautéed mushrooms. Sprinkle with a few thyme leaves and toasted hazelnuts to garnish.

Index

ACKNOWLEDGEMENTS

I will look back on this book and the recipes within it with fondness for many years to come. I am in my infancy when it comes to growing food, farming and rediscovering lost knowledge of free and wild foods. There's so much more to come and I think this book really is a giant stepping stone on my journey to a totally self-sufficient lifestyle. It's really nice to track my progress through books and I'm so grateful to have the opportunity to write them. As a young, skinny, 16-year-old chef working his ass off, I honestly would never have believed I'd be an author to multiple books.

Firstly, I want to thank my mum and dad. I am only able to do everything I love because of the foundation you gave me as I grew up. You did everything you could to give Charlotte and me the best possible start. To this day, you're always so helpful with all of my endeavours. I love you both so much. Charlotte, my lovely sister – as you're settling down, I hope these recipes become some of your new favourites (and you finally realize how cool growing food is!). I love you!

Over the 8 years that I have been making videos on my YouTube channel and social media, I've developed from nervously standing behind my kitchen counter making recipes, to now documenting beautiful stories through food. I want to share the biggest thank you to my best friend and colleague Tom, for the unbelievable effort and creativity that has gone into crafting these films with me. I cannot wait for our future expeditions around the world and the videos we'll make. I was nervous to take on the responsibility of shooting the whole book at my house (having previously shot every other book I've done with my good friend Simon Smith at his dedicated food photography studio), but with our creativity I knew we could do it. Tom, thank you – you're the kindest, sweetest and most creative human! Thank you for everything.

During the shoot, we had additional help shooting the photos from my long-time friend Oliver Biggs, who mastered the lighting brilliantly. Ollie, we couldn't have shot the photos so nicely without you and I can't thank you enough for all your hard work over the years. Finally, to Matt, thanks for capturing the cover image – you really nailed that one!

To Emma, Caitlin and Lu, thanks so much for all your effort preparing the food for the shoot. It was an intense schedule but you were a much-needed sense of calm each day. Thank you for all of the creativity and passion you put in! Thank you also to Luis for sourcing the most beautiful backgrounds and props that matched my home perfectly.

Teigan, I want to thank you so much for being my rock and always being there. You're so selfless, creative and caring. I can't wait to see where the future takes us and how vibrant the garden we grow together becomes.

To everyone at Quadrille who has helped make this book happen, thank you. Sarah – I really appreciate the vote of confidence in me, and that you gave me the opportunity to write another book. It means the world. Stacey, Emily and Harriet – thank you for bearing with me, for putting up with my creative demands and working so tirelessly to bring this book together. Thank you!

I really would love again to thank all the people who inspired and encouraged me to start growing food. I mention them at the start of the book, so please go and check them out if this book gives you the nudge to start growing food of your own.

Thank you to my long-time agents Zoe and Olivia – you work so hard for me and have helped create opportunities I could only dream of. Thanks for always supporting me.

Finally, to each and every one of you who bought this book, I can't thank you enough. It really does mean the world.

ABOUT THE AUTHOR

Gaz Oakley is passionate about plants. After becoming a chef in Cardiff, UK, at the age of just 15, he was inspired to switch up his diet, using the techniques he learned working as a professional chef to devise delicious, innovative dishes with plants at the heart of the plate. Gaz now has over 3 million followers on social media and his previous three books (*Vegan 100*, *Plants Only Kitchen* and *Plants Only Holidays*) were instant hits worldwide.

Quadrille, Penguin Random House UK, One Embassy Gardens, 8 Viaduct Gardens, London SW11 7BW

Quadrille Publishing Limited is part of the Penguin Random House group of companies whose addresses can be found at global. penguinrandomhouse.com

Penguin
Random House
UK

Published by Quadrille in 2025

www.penguin.co.uk

A CIP catalogue record for this book is available from the British Library

ISBN 978-1-83783-292-7
10 9 8 7 6 5 4 3 2 1

Managing Director
Sarah Lavelle

Senior Commissioning Editor
Stacey Cleworth

Project Editor
Harriet Webster

Copy Editors
Sally Somers & Harriet Webster

Art Direction and Design
Emily Lapworth

Photographers
Tom Kong, Gaz Oakley, Oliver Biggs & Matthew Williams

Cover Photographer
Matthew Williams

Lighting
Oliver Biggs

Food Stylists
Emma Cantlay & Gaz Oakley

Food Stylist Assistants
Caitlin Macdonald & Lucy Cottle

Prop Stylists
Luis Peral & Gaz Oakley

Production Manager
Sabeena Atchia

Colour reproduction by F1

Printed in China by C&C Offset Printing Co., Ltd.

The authorised representative in the EEA is Penguin Random House Ireland, Morrison Chambers, 32 Nassau Street, Dublin D02 YH68.

Penguin Random House is committed to a sustainable future for our business, our readers and our planet. This book is made from Forest Stewardship Council® certified paper.